Sources of Wealth

AN EASY GUIDE TO MAKING YOUR MONEY GROW

By
Andrea Plos

Copyright © 2013 Andrea Plos

All rights reserved.

ISBN: 978-0-9888380-0-0

Dedication

This book is dedicated to my beloved wife, Laura, who has spent the last 14 years by my side. I hope I will deserve to have you with me for the rest of my life.

To my dog, Judith, because you love me no matter what!

To my best friends:

- *Paolo, because I've become successful without either taking your advice or ending up in jail.*
- *Barbara, because every time I asked you whether I should follow my dreams, you smiled and said, "Go for it!"*
- *Carolina, because you can read the future for all of us and I want you to be part of it. And because Laura picks you to go with her to Muse concerts so I can stay home!*

To Justine and Sharon, because this book would not be possible without you.

Contents

About the author	i
Foreword	ii
Introduction	v
How to use this book	v
PART 1 – THE KEY TO A SUCCESSFUL MINDSET	1
Chapter 1: Change Your Mindset	4
Steps for positive thinking	4
Chapter 2: Seeing the Bigger Picture	7
Rules for positive thinking	8
- Try this: Count your blessings	8
Dealing with setbacks	8
Learning from failure	9
Chapter 3: Knowing What You Really Want	10
Create an action plan	11
Some rules for goal setting	11
10 Rules to Remember	12
PART 2 – A BEGINNER'S GUIDE TO FINANCE	13
Two ways to make money	15
Chapter 4: Speculating vs. Investing	16
Speculating	16
Investing	17
The difference between investing and speculating	17
Why speculation goes wrong	18
- A little history lesson	18
- The tulip bulb craze	18
- The South Sea bubble	19
- The Wall Street Crash	20
- The dot-com bubble	20
- Why did it go so wrong?	21
Chapter 5: Basic Concepts for Investing	23
Before you invest ...	23
Types of investment	23
Investing to generate multiple streams of income	24
- Income and your goals	24

- Short-term savings	24
- Long-term savings	24
- Modern portfolio theory	25
- Minimizing risk by creating a portfolio	26
Risk	27
What type of investor are you?	28
- The two types of investor	28
- Defensive and aggressive investment game plans	28
- Quick tips for choosing an investment	29
- Weighing the risk	29
10 Rules to Remember	31
PART 3 – BUILDING YOUR ASSETS	**31**
Chapter 6: An Introduction to Types of Assets	**32**
Bank accounts	32
- Interest rates	32
- Types of bank accounts	33
Bonds	34
- Coupons, yields, and prices explained	35
- Types of bond	38
Real Estate	38
- Why is Real Estate a good investment?	39
- Where do I start?	39
- Getting start-up capital	40
- The costs of Real Estate	41
Chapter 7: Stocks and Shares	**43**
The Stock Market	43
- Primary and secondary markets	44
Indexes	44
- Some key indexes	44
Profiting from Shares	44
- Types of shares	45
The benefits of owning shares	46
- Some rules for investing in shares	46
- How much does it cost to own shares?	46
Buying shares	47
Assets at a Glance	49
Chapter 8: Three Investment Strategies	**50**
Matching assets to your goals	50

Chapter 9: Paying Tax on Your Assets — 53
Dividends tax — 53
Capital gains tax — 53
  - Paying capital gains and dividends tax — 54
Chapter 10: Financial Advisors — 55
Types of financial advisors — 55
5 Rules to Remember — 57
PART 4 – "IT'S COMPLICATED" – TECHNIQUES THE PROS USE — 58
Where the experts failed — 60
Chapter 11: Basic Principles — 61
Firm foundation theory — 61
  - Determining intrinsic value — 61
Castle-in-the-air theory — 62
Chapter 12: Predicting the Future — 64
Foolish prediction techniques — 64
More sensible techniques — 64
  - Technical Analysis — 65
  - Fundamental Analysis — 65
How technical analysis works — 65
  - The pros and cons of charting — 66
Fundamental Analysis — 67
  - How to use fundamental analysis — 68
A final word — 69
3 Rules to Remember — 70
PART 5 – A PRACTICAL GUIDE FOR INVESTORS — 71
Getting into practice — 72
Chapter 13: Before You Invest ... — 73
Assessing your ability to handle risk — 73
Build your safety net — 74
  - Cash reserves — 75
  - Why save? — 75
  - Beating inflation — 77
Insurance — 78
  - Life insurance — 79
  - Choosing the right insurance plan — 79
10 Rules to Remember — 80
Chapter 14: Choosing Your Assets — 81
Assets according to risk — 82

Chapter 15: Building Your Investment Portfolio — 83
Example portfolios for each age group — 83
- 20s — 83
- 30s / 40s — 83
- 50s — 84
- 60s — 85
Rebalancing your portfolio — 85
5 Rules to Remember — 86

Chapter 16: Getting the Most out of Shares — 87
Index funds — 87
- The advantages of index funds — 87
- Choosing your funds — 88
- Reduce risk by diversifying — 89
- Indexes to go by — 90
Index funds at a glance — 90

Chapter 17: Choosing Your Own Shares — 91
Where to find out more — 92
- Newspapers and journals — 92
- Advisory services — 92

Chapter 18: Professional Management — 93
The advantages of active management — 93
The disadvantages of active management — 94
The costs explained — 94
- Fees — 94
- Expense charges — 95
Recap: The Three Methods of Buying Stocks — 96

Chapter 19: Real Estate — 97
Understanding the Market — 97
- External influencing factors — 98
- Making the most of the current trend — 98
5 Rules to Remember — 99

Chapter 20: Achieving Your Goals through Smart Investing — 100
Goal number 1: Saving for college — 100
- Zero coupon bonds — 101
- 529 savings account — 101
Goal number 2: Buying a home — 102
- Money-market mutual funds — 103
- Example savings portfolio — 104

Goal number 3: Planning for retirement	104
- Individual Retirement Accounts (IRAs)	105
- Roth IRAs	105
Pension plans	105
- If you're in employment	105
- If you're self-employed	105
A final word	106
PART 6 – STARTING YOUR OWN BUSINESS	108
Chapter 21: The 80/20 Principle	111
Using the 80/20 principle in your business	111
- Getting into good habits	112
- Time management	112
6 Rules for success	113
Recap: The 80/20 Principle	114
Chapter 22: Bricks and Mortar – How a Business Is Constructed	115
Your mission	115
Your team	116
Systems management	116
Leadership	116
Communication	117
Cash flow	117
Chapter 23: Building a Successful Business	118
The five components of a successful business	118
- Value creation	119
- Marketing	119
The golden rule	119
- Sales	119
- Value delivery	119
- Financial security	119
Value creation – Finding your niche	120
- How to evaluate a market	120
Weighing up the risks	121
- SWOT analysis	121
- Cost / Benefit analysis	123
Rules to remember	123
Marketing	125
- Building your brand	125

Warning:	124
- Deciding on your style	127
Blowing your own trumpet	127
Marketing's golden rules	128
Using different channels	129
- Online	129
- "Above the line"	130
Making a sale	130
Going on autopilot	132
Financial security	133
- Defining pricing to make a profit	134
Chapter 24: Becoming a Leader	135
Rules for good leadership	135
- Avoid criticism and blame	135
- Put yourself in their shoes	135
- Call people by name	135
- Compromise	135
- Empathize	136
- Give a reason for your actions	136
Rules to remember for a successful business	138
- Value creation	138
- Marketing	138
- Sales	138
- Going on autopilot	138
- Financial security	138
- Leadership	138
A final word	138
PART 7 – WHERE TO FIND OUT MORE	140
Daily papers	141
Weekly papers/magazines	141
Advisory services	142
Mutual funds	142
Emerging market mutual funds	143
Insurance comparison	143
Bank comparisons	144
Government securities	144
Tax	144

About the author

Andrea Plos is a serial entrepreneur and investor with more than 20 years' experience in finance. A former marketing manager in a large international bank, he was also a sales executive for a Fortune 500 firm.

Andrea is now the founder of successful multi-million-dollar businesses in mobile applications, retail, and commercial Real Estate and consultancy.

Foreword

It's safe to say that if I can make it, anyone can. You don't need to be born into a wealthy family or be the brightest kid in school. I certainly wasn't. I was hardly a brilliant scholar, and my childhood was difficult thanks to my mother's long illness and my father's absence.

But despite these early setbacks, I now have a wonderful wife whom I love with all my heart, a small group of close friends whom I love to spend my free time with, and enough money to ensure that my family and I can live comfortably. I guess you could say I've made it.

Today, I own houses in some of Europe's most beautiful locations and work with a group of talented and energetic business partners who have helped me become rich. I've helped them, too. Right now, I couldn't ask for more, but remember—I didn't start off with wealth and privilege on my side.

In this book, I'll share my secret to success with you. Quite simply, I believe that you can achieve whatever you want. You just need to know how to do it.

Sounds easy, doesn't it? In actual fact, it is! Everything you need to know is out there, waiting for you to come and grab it and make it your own.

Let me explain.

In the early 2000s I was unhappy. I was young. I had a good job and a successful career ahead of me, but I felt deeply that I was missing something important. I soon realized what it was—*time*—quality time that I could spend with my family and friends, doing what I love.

I realized that if I continued as I was, my life would be over in a flash and I would be old before I'd had a chance to enjoy myself. In my imagination, I saw the next 30 years—each day passing predictably and without excitement until the time came for me to retire. I had been sleepwalking through my life, and the time had come to make a radical change.

I asked myself how I could change my life into the life I wanted. What I really wanted was more free time—but to achieve that with any level of security, I would need to become wealthy.

I said to myself, "With money I will buy time to do the things I love. Jewels and fast cars are pleasant side effects, but really I want to use my money to enrich the lives of the people I love and make other people happier." I decided that money was neither good nor bad in itself, but it does give people the power to amplify their good or bad qualities. If you are a good person, money can help you achieve a more positive impact in the world than you would be able to otherwise.

I wanted to make a lot of money. And for me, the best way to achieve this was to learn "the rules." Every aspect of life has rules, and money is no exception. Come to grips with those rules and you can become very, very rich.

Think about it for a second: Every day, billions of dollars are traded on the stock market. Money is not a scarce commodity—it's everywhere, being exchanged in huge quantities every day. You need only to know how where to look for it.

So I studied. A lot. But no one becomes rich by reading books without applying their knowledge, so I put my newfound wisdom to work. To my disappointment, nothing happened and the strategies that seemed so simple on paper didn't yield the result I wanted.

I decided to find a mentor. With his help, I've made three vital discoveries on my journey to wealth:

1. Follow in the footsteps of those who are already rich, not those who want to become rich. Is your banker, broker, or advisor rich? If he isn't, he probably can't teach you much.
2. Focus on your financial education and try to learn as much as you can. Evaluate every opportunity yourself.
3. Try to understand financial trends—but don't follow them.

In this book I've tried to combine the basics I've learnt in these years with some advice and hints that may help. Consider it a starting point on your journey to wealth—a small spring that develops into a large river with every passing day. Just as a small river becomes bigger and bigger as smaller streams flow into it, your knowledge will grow as you continue your financial education.

I hope this book helps you start your journey. Keep an open mind, learn all you can, and good luck!

Andrea

Introduction

For many people, the subject of finance is scary stuff. Mention investments, stocks, shares, or bonds and they run for the hills. It doesn't have to be that way. Everyone has the power to take their finances into their own hands and gain greater control over their lives. With this book, I aim to help you do just that.

This book is a no-nonsense, easy-to-follow guide for everyone who has ever been afraid of finance. In it you'll find the tools to help you grow your money and increase your peace of mind, and you'll find the confidence to achieve the things you've always dreamed of.

With a little research and commitment, everyone can make their money work harder for them. You don't need special skills or particular talents to become rich. You just need to follow some simple rules for success—rules you'll discover in this book. And with the right attitude, you'll discover how to grow your money easily.

How to use this book

In this book, you will learn about the different types of investment—from paper assets to Real Estate, as well as how to assess and manage risk, set achievable goals, and even start your own business. We'll meet some successful people and examine the decisions they made that helped them achieve success—including the skills they developed, which sectors they invested in, and how they approached the opportunities and problems that came their way.

Two of the most vital lessons you will learn are how to approach life with a positive attitude and how to develop the skills to handle whatever challenges come your way with confidence and ease. This is what Part 1 is all about. We'll discover the key to a successful mindset and how to change the negative beliefs that hold you back from achieving your goals.

In Part 2, we'll introduce you to some basic concepts behind investing, including risk, multiple streams of income, and the difference between speculation and investment.

Part 3 covers everything from different types of assets (which give you income) to the liabilities (costs) that come with these assets. We'll introduce you to the stock market and some of the financial advisors that can help or hinder you along the way.

Part 4 delves into some of the theories the experts use—and why they don't always deliver. Financial professionals love to try and predict the market—to determine which companies will grow; which will decline; and what products, projects, or firms will be "the next big thing." Once you understand the theories, you can judge for yourself whether they're any good.

Part 5 is a practical guide to investing. It's for everyone, whether you're young or old, wealthy or not. Everyone can benefit from allocating their money properly and starting a program of regular savings. You don't have to be rich to get rich.

You'll learn about starting your own business in Part 6. It's a wonderfully rewarding way to earn income and leaves you free to be your own boss. When it comes to starting your own business, there are pitfalls to avoid and skills to learn, which is where we step in with some helpful hints to get you started off on the right foot.

Finally, at the end of the book, we'll point you in the direction of financial papers, books, magazines, and websites that can give you the information you need to make the most informed choice about your investments.

And finally...

It is possible for everyone to grow their money successfully. With the right information and the right mindset, you can lead a better life, make better decisions, and reap the rewards of your investment. It's a lot of fun, too! This book gives you the tools to help you move forward confidently and powerfully, achieve your goals, and kill your fear of finance once and for all.

We hope you enjoy the journey!

PART 1

THE KEY TO A SUCCESSFUL MINDSET

*The pessimist sees difficulty in every opportunity.
The optimist sees the opportunity in every difficulty.*

– Winston Churchill

Money is a powerful thing. It offers security in old age, a better future for our children, and a helping hand in times of crisis. It can bring respect, influence, and authority.

Living without money in 21st-century America is very difficult. Certain expenses are unavoidable—renting an apartment, medical bills, and transportation are just a few—and that's before taking things like college education into account.

The lack of money can induce fear and even panic. If you don't have much money, perhaps you prefer not to think about it at all.

This book brings the hope that IT DOESN'T HAVE TO BE LIKE THAT. Let me stress that. You have the power to change your situation. You are not stuck in a rut even if it feels as if you are. Commit this to memory:

> *It is possible for **everyone**, no matter how little money they start with, to increase their wealth and be successful.*

Don't believe me? Let me introduce you to someone who achieved just that.

In 1960s Milwaukee, a 13-year-old girl ran away from home after suffering years of abuse. She was sent to a juvenile detention center, only to be denied entry because there was no available space. Eventually, she moved to Nashville to live with her father, and at age 17 was hired by WVOL radio as a part-time news reporter.

> *A keen actress and a dedicated worker, she moved to Baltimore, eventually winning a spot as co-anchor for the WJ2-TV News team.*
>
> *That little girl—Oprah Winfrey—became the host of the highest-rated talk show in television history. From difficult beginnings, Oprah became a household name and was estimated to be the richest African-American of the 20th century. It is thanks to Oprah's patience and determination in the face of hardship that she enjoys her success.*

Oprah's story is particularly special, but the fact is that every single day people from humble beginnings establish themselves in the world thanks to their hard work, patience, and self-belief in the face of all odds.

You can learn those skills too. By using simple, sensible tactics, you too can grow your wealth and achieve your ambitions slowly but surely. There will be difficulties along the way, but you can easily overcome them with the right mental attitude.

Chapter 1

Change Your Mindset

It is never too late to be what you might have been.
– George Eliot

Your mind is a powerful thing. It's as malleable and changeable as a muscle and has a huge capacity for growth and development. Just because you believe that you aren't good at something doesn't mean you can't be—you can learn what you don't know, and you can develop skills you don't currently possess.

Successful people aren't always the ones who are naturally gifted. They are the ones who don't let their weaknesses stand in the way. They try to overcome them instead.

Steps for positive thinking

1. Set a vision for the future.

You can't hit a target you can't see, so decide what you want and make goals to help you get there. Be optimistic and don't be afraid to dream. Imagine yourself successful, confident, and unafraid, then color in that happy vision with as many details as you can. Make it vivid, and reinforce it every day.

2. Identify your strengths and build on your weaknesses.

Your weaknesses aren't permanent. Decide which areas of your life you would like to improve and commit to practicing them.

3. Take each day as it comes.

Do the best that you can each day. Some days will be better than others, but if you make a commitment to do the best you can for that day, you will start to see an improvement.

4. Believe in yourself.

You are constantly changing and full of potential. Recognize it and build on it—don't let other people's lack of enthusiasm impact your self-belief.

5. Build a positive outlook.

The brain isn't hardwired to be a certain way, but your habitual thoughts have a huge molding influence on your outlook in life. If your thoughts are often negative, you are programming your brain to spot negative patterns and improving its capacity for negativity. Make an effort to think more positively and challenge your automatic, negative thoughts when they cross your mind. With time, you will start to train your brain toward a more positive state.

6. Feel the fear and do it anyway.

Any new experience, whether it's making an investment for the first time or learning to drive, can be scary. Do your homework, assess the risks, and then take action. Putting it off won't make it any less scary, but if you take the plunge, you may find you had nothing to fear.

7. Choose your friends wisely.

Research suggests that you are the average of the five people you spend the most time with. Socialize with people you admire—find out what makes them successful and imitate their positive qualities. If your social circle isn't supporting your goals, change it!

8. Work on honesty and integrity.

It takes years to build trust, and only a moment to destroy it. Think about how you want to be seen by the people you value and keep yourself worthy of their trust.

9. Take action.

There will never be "the perfect time" for any action. Consider your options, make a decision, and act on that decision. Time is precious, so make yours productive.

10. Set limits.

It's a well-known phenomenon that any task will expand to fill the time available. Set yourself time limits to accomplish a goal and stick to them; otherwise, work will consume all your energy.

11. Get into good habits.

Habits are exceptionally powerful. Try setting yourself a challenge—getting up early in the morning, for example—and keep at it for 20 days. It will soon become second nature.

Chapter 2

Seeing the Bigger Picture

There has been much tragedy in my life; at least half of it actually happened.
– Mark Twain

You may have heard the expression "you are what you think." It's certainly true that our thoughts have a powerful influence over the way we feel, and most of our negative thoughts are actually unwarranted.

This is particularly true in a situation with an uncertain outcome—like going for a job interview, for example. It's natural to imagine the worst ("I'll be late," or "They'll never hire me anyway, what's the point in even attending?")—but don't. In many cases, your fears are unfounded. Allowing them space in your thoughts sabotages your state of mind and affects your performance as a result.

Of course, bad things do happen sometimes, and you cannot always avoid difficult situations, but you can minimize their negative impact by thinking positively.

Many of us blow our worries out of proportion, particularly where money is concerned. If you don't have much money, it can feel like the end of the world. In reality, it isn't. Rather than comparing yourself with the richest people on the planet, try comparing yourself with:

- The 15.6 million Americans who suffer extreme poverty, or
- The 25,000 people who die from hunger or problems related to it every day.

Now that you've made those comparisons, does your situation feel so bleak?

Rules for positive thinking

Positive thinking doesn't mean blind optimism. It means taking into account the positive things going on in your life and being grateful for them. By focusing on the things that are going well rather than those that aren't, you can develop your brain to think in a way that makes you more likely to see the positives in any situation, whether good or bad.

This can help you deal with setbacks and overcome problems when they occur.

Try this: Count your blessings

Get into the habit of thinking about the good stuff. Count your blessings. Every day, make a list of five things that have gone well for you and that you can be grateful for. They don't have to be big things—anything that makes you happy will do. Here's an example:

1. The sun was shining.
2. I made it to work early today.
3. My partner and I shared a joke.
4. I had a delicious meal for lunch.
5. A friend invited me to dinner next week.

Dealing with setbacks

Making decisions about your finances and deciding how to manage your investments means taking risks. When things go wrong, it's natural to feel worried and upset, and the negatives can feel overwhelming. But in reality, things aren't always as bad as they seem.

Look at the following table. It records an event, the negative thoughts that might come with it, and some plausible, more positive, alternative thoughts.

Event	What I thought	Alternative thoughts
Losing a job	- I'm obviously not cut out for this. - I'll never get another job. - I'm a failure.	- The company has been having difficulties. This isn't necessarily a reflection on my performance. - Perhaps I would be better suited to a different job. - I'll find another position that makes me happier.

Now try creating a similar table for setbacks you have dealt with. Do they still seem as bad?

Learning from failure

Most people dislike failing at a task and do their best to avoid situations where they fail. But "failing" to achieve something isn't always a bad thing. Failure can teach us much more than success can: If we open our minds to consider why we might have failed, we can figure out what to change so that we can do it better next time.

> ## Failure doesn't always mean it's over
>
> One successful businessman who is no stranger to failure is Donald Trump. Now he is the CEO of Trump Organization, a Real Estate development company, and a billionaire as well. But a few years ago, things looked very different for him.
>
> By 1989, poor business decisions left Donald Trump unable to meet loan payments, and two years later his business was bankrupt. Banks and bond holders opted to restructure his debt, despite having lost hundreds of millions of dollars, in order to avoid a costly lawsuit.
>
> Trump unearthed some of his earlier projects and not only made good the losses he sustained, he made a considerable profit. He is now worth an estimated $5 billion.

Chapter 3

Knowing What You Really Want

The trouble with not having a goal is that you can spend your life running up and down the field and never score.
– Bill Copeland

What do you really want? Answering that question can be more difficult than it seems, but it's important to establish what your true goals are if you are to have a chance of meeting them.

One trick is to make a statement—for example, "I want to be rich"—and ask five follow-up questions to interrogate your first assumption. Here's how it works:

"I want to be rich."

- Why do I want to be rich? – I don't want to worry about money.
- Why don't I want to worry about money? – I don't want to be afraid.
- Why don't I want to be afraid? – I want to feel secure.
- Why do I want to feel secure? – I want to feel free.
- Why do I want to feel free? – I want to be free.

The last question has brought you to the root of your actual desire. The goal isn't to be rich but to be free. The next stage is determining how you can become free. You might:

- Pay off an outstanding debt
- Work less, find a different job, or become an entrepreneur
- Move to a new city or country
- Break off a relationship that is too restricting

Create an action plan

Having identified your goals, it's time to act. Each of the goals listed above is daunting in itself, so you'll need to break them down into achievable, specific, measurable steps. Creating a written plan is a great way to ensure you are meeting your goals, plus it will help you measure your progress and stay on track. Here's how to set goals:

1. Write down your main goal or project (e.g., get out of debt).
2. Write down the expected outcome as a single sentence. Identify what it is that needs to happen before you can say your project is complete (e.g., have some money saved at the end of the month).
3. Identify the first action you need to complete to move closer to your goal (e.g., make small cutbacks—reduce coffees at Starbucks, eat packed lunch at work instead of lunch out, etc.).
4. When you've completed the first action, write down another one (e.g., pay bills on time, cut credit cards, grow your income, start an emergency fund—use saved money from step 3 aiming to collect $1,000).
5. Repeat the process as often as you need, focusing on one action at a time (e.g., pay bills on time, cut credit cards, grow your income, etc.).

Some rules for goal setting

- Goals should be positive. "I want to be rich" is better than "I don't want to be poor."
- Goals should be immediate. Include an action you can start today.
- Keep them concrete. Goals need to be measurable with results you can see in the real world. "I want to be happy" is not a concrete goal. You need to identify some signs that will let you know you've achieved your goal.
- Goals need to be specific. A specific goal defines what, where, and when you will achieve it. "I want to be financially free in five years' time" is a specific goal.

10 Rules to Remember

1. *It is possible for **everyone** to grow their wealth, no matter how little they start with.*
2. *You have the power to change your situation.*
3. *Your weaknesses aren't permanent. Aim to develop your skills so that your weaknesses become strengths.*
4. *You are what you think. Build a positive outlook—banish negative thoughts and assumptions.*
5. *Just because you feel something, doesn't make it true.*
6. *Don't put off until tomorrow what can be done today.*
7. *Live with integrity.*
8. *Imitate people you admire.*
9. *Decide what you really want.*
10. *Set measurable, specific, achievable goals for yourself.*

PART 2

A BEGINNER'S GUIDE TO FINANCE

The man who removes a mountain begins by carrying away small stones.

– Chinese proverb

A financial education can open a great number of doors, and being financially literate will help you spot opportunities that could benefit you. A little extra wisdom never hurt anyone—in fact, knowing your stuff when it comes to finance can only increase your options when it comes to gaining wealth.

In this part you will learn:

- ✓ How to earn money through multiple streams of income
- ✓ What risks are involved in investing
- ✓ The difference between investing and speculation
- ✓ The three main investment strategies

Generally, people who fail to become rich do so because they fear losing money or because they don't believe it's possible. They might have deeply held habits which they allow to control their behavior, or they may be unwilling to re-educate themselves.

Those who do become rich feel fear but don't hold back because of it. They focus on what they want, rather than what they can't have, and they are open to learning new things when they lack expertise.

Walt Disney's story

As a young man, Walt Disney had a hard time getting a job. He was fired from an early news reporter position because he "lacked imagination and had no good ideas," and his subsequent start-up business ventures were similarly unlucky, ending miserably in failure and bankruptcy on more than one occasion.

His luck began to turn when he got a job with the Kansas City Film Ad Company, making commercials based on cut-out animations. The company owner lent him a camera to experiment with his own animations, which lead to Disney's decision to open his own animation business focusing on cel animation. The cartoons became very popular throughout Kansas, and soon Disney started to establish a following.

Today, Disney is a world-famous brand and an industry worth several billion dollars. But its founder had to learn a few hard lessons before he could achieve success.

Disney didn't give up in the face of failure and rejection. Instead, he turned his focus toward an area that interested him and developed the skills he was missing so that he could deliver a product that the public loved.

Two ways to make money

Regardless of how much you start with, when it comes to making money, you have two basic options. You can either earn more of it, or you can make your money work for you by investing it in companies or projects that you expect to make a profit.

In the first instance, you increase your income by changing jobs, working longer hours, or achieving a promotion to earn a higher salary. You deposit your money in a savings account where it earns a small percentage of interest each year.

In the second instance, the idea is that by investing your money rather than depositing it in a savings account, your funds increase by themselves.

When you deposit money in a bank, the lump sum won't appreciate in real terms. It might earn interest (which may or may not keep up with inflation), but it won't make you any extra cash. It may even lose purchasing power if inflation is higher than the interest you receive.

Chapter 4

Speculating vs. Investing

When it comes to making money, there are two main options: speculating, or investing. There's a big difference between the two, and investment is by far the safer strategy. In the long term, investment will always generate better returns than speculating (or "trading") will. Despite this, speculation is still popular with many would-be investors, which is why it's important to examine the dangers here.

Let's take a quick look at the two methods:

Speculating

Speculators buy stocks when the prices are low and try to sell them to other investors at a profit. They rely on market fluctuations to buy stocks when their values are low and to sell them when the values rise. Timing and guesswork are the main watchwords for speculators, who keep a close eye on the markets to try and anticipate which shares will grow in value fastest.

Because speculation is based upon the minute and ever-changing fluctuations of the market, the outcome can never be certain. The speculator relies on his ability to find other investors who are willing to buy his stocks at their inflated price. He tries to beat the same market that he's contributing to—which means he's trying to beat other speculators who know as much about the market as he does.

Speculators believe in a phenomenon known as the **"greater fool" theory**. The idea is that there will always be someone stupid enough to jump on the bandwagon when stock prices start to rise. As long as you can anticipate when they will fall again, and as long as there is someone stupider than you to take the fall, you can't lose.

Investing

Put simply, investment means putting money into a project or a company that you believe—after thorough research—to have a strong likelihood of future success and growth.

Investors acquire securities, such as company shares and bonds, which have a good chance of appreciating in value in the medium to long term. They focus on sound, well-managed companies whose true value is distinct from the fluctuations of share prices.

For the investor, changes in the market have a less profound effect on the earning potential of his investment because it is based upon fundamentals such as the good management and long-term success of the company.

The difference between investing and speculating

SPECULATING	INVESTING
Advantages: - Sudden fluctuations in the market mean it's possible to make a lot of money very quickly. - High risk means high returns. *Disadvantages:* - It is impossible to predict the market accurately enough to guarantee consistent results. - Speculators need to guess right 70% of the time just to break even. - It's easy to lose large sums of money.	*Advantages:* - Long-term investments tend to perform better than short-term trading on the stock market. - Risk is more manageable. - Investors rely less on the stupidity of others for their gains. *Disadvantages:* - Lower-risk investments mean lower possible returns. - It takes longer to generate income than a single lucky speculation.

Why speculation goes wrong

> *It is the mark of an educated man to be able to entertain a thought without accepting it.*
> *– Albert Einstein.*

In case I have not convinced you of the dangers of speculation, the following are some examples from history where speculation has gone dramatically wrong.

When it comes to the stock market, the only way you're going to be able to reliably tell which stocks will rise and which will fall is by getting in your time machine and travelling back a few years, armed with the index figures from the financial papers from every subsequent week. Other than that, there's simply no way to be certain, 100% of the time, which stocks will perform better than others.

This doesn't mean that people don't try to do exactly that. Ever since trading in securities began in the 12th century in France, there have been plenty of tales of woe relating to the hapless hopefuls who tried to predict the market. Get it right, and the rewards can be immense. Get it wrong, and the consequences are disastrous.

A little history lesson

Sometimes, someone will come up with an idea, or design a product, that seems so spectacularly wonderful that the public goes mad for it. Imagine being one of the first people to invest in Google, for example.

Excitement mounts as more and more people buy shares in this particular company or invest in that particular scheme. The madness of crowds takes over and a bubble forms. But bubbles can't last forever. They burst when it becomes apparent that the market value far outweighs the stock's true value. One by one, the key players sell out, the rest follow suit, and the stock plummets.

The tulip bulb craze

In early 17th-century Holland, a botany professor brought some unusual plants from Turkey to Leyden. He placed a high price on these unique plants. No one bought them, but one night a thief broke into the professor's home and stole the lot. In the course of the next decade, these exotic tulips became extremely popular in Dutch gardens. Bulb merchants tried to predict the most popular colors and varieties for the coming year in order to charge higher prices, and as their popularity rose, so too did the prices. Before long, people considered tulips a smart investment.

Word spread and people cottoned on to the trend. Confident that prices would continue to rise, the crowds continued to buy the bulbs. And rise they did—by a staggering 20 times their original value during January 1637. At this stage, prudent investors decided it would be a good idea to sell—a decision that was quickly echoed by the majority of investors. By February, panic reigned, people fought to sell their shares, and the stock plummeted. Thousands of people lost their original investments as tulip bulbs quickly became almost worthless in the market's eyes.

The South Sea bubble

England in the 18th century was in a good spot, financially. A long period of prosperity had resulted in large savings—which the public were ready to squander. In 1711, the South Sea Company was formed in a bid to restore faith in the government's ability to keep its promises. The company took on government debt of £10 million in exchange for a trading monopoly over the South Seas.

Because of its sheer confidence in assuming such a high level of debt, as well as the perceived trading benefits from its unrestricted access to the South Seas, word quickly spread that the South Sea Company could make millions.

But there was a snag. Unbeknownst to the public, not a single director of the company had the slightest experience in South American trade. What's more, several of the directors were happily defrauding the public: Holders of government securities, which would be assumed by the South Sea Company, swapped their government securities for shares in the company. Meanwhile, those in the company bought up government securities for £55 on the quiet and re-sold them as South Sea stock for twice that amount.

The whole thing was a castle in the air—a costly, ruinously high-maintenance façade with no foundation in terms of what the company was actually worth. Desperate to keep up appearances, the company rented an impressive London house as their "headquarters." In 1720, the directors offered to fund the *entire national debt*, which stood at £31 million. Impressed by such brazen confidence, the public continued to invest and the stock rose from £130 to £300 in just a few days.

Inspired by the South Sea Company's success, would-be entrepreneurs advanced absurd new financing proposals in the hope of persuading investors to empty their pockets. The projects ranged from trading in human hair to extracting sunlight from cucumbers—and all over the country people queued up to hand over their money.

Eventually, realizing that the South Sea Company's market value bore no resemblance to the real prospects of the company, the directors quietly sold out. Once the news leaked, the stock plummeted, leaving thousands of investors bereft.

The Wall Street Crash

Perhaps the most famous bubble of the 20th century was the Wall Street Crash. The "Roaring Twenties" were a time of excess, and rising prices in the stock market seemed to confirm this financial confidence. Over six years, the Dow Jones Industrial Average had increased fivefold in value, peaking on September 3, 1929. The market's rising trend looked to be permanent.

On October 24 (Black Thursday), the trend abruptly ended. The market lost 11% of its value at the opening bell. Extensive newspaper coverage was followed by an exodus from the market on Monday, October 28, with a further loss of 13%. The following day William C. Durant and members of the Rockefeller family bucked the trend and bought large quantities of stocks to demonstrate their faith in the market, but their efforts could not stop the landslide. By the evening, the market had lost over $30 billion in the space of two days.

The dot-com bubble

Many bubbles are associated with some sort of new technology and the Internet is no exception. In 2000, the Internet represented exciting new business opportunities and was the subject of widespread (and very positive) media coverage. These positive feedback loops led to big profits for early stockholders, who spread the word about their success at glitzy parties. Naturally, envious party guests wanted a piece of the pie and invested too.

In the early 2000s, expectations of future returns on dot-com stock ranged from 15–25%, or even higher. Cisco, a big hitter in the technological industry, was selling at a three-digit multiple of earnings and had a market capitalization of almost $600 billion. A continued return of 15% per year for the next 25 years would have made this company bigger than the entire economy, but there was a huge rift between actual value and perceived value.

All over the world, people jumped on the bandwagon. Witnessing the success of technological firms, a plethora of new firms sporting "dot com" or "tronics" as part of their branding appeared in the market indexes. The change of name was well thought out—companies whose names suggested a technological bent were selling shares at almost double the value of non-technological companies.

Unfortunately, rising prices led to fraudulent practices. Most famously, Enron massively overstated its earnings following a joint venture with Blockbuster to make it possible to rent movies online. The deal failed some months later, but Enron still borrowed $115 million from a Canadian bank in exchange for future profits from the Blockbuster deal. That particular venture made zero profits, but Enron still counted the bank loan as a profit, artificially inflating its earnings and pushing the perceived value of its stock still higher. In 2001, Enron went bankrupt, leaving employees without jobs or their retirement savings. (It had offered pension plans consisting entirely of Enron shares.) In 2006, Enron's top executives Ken Lay and Jeff Skilling were convicted of conspiracy and fraud.

Why did it go so wrong?

So what happened to make everything go so wrong? Surely not everyone could have been stupid enough to believe that prices would rise forever?

No. Most people would not have been that stupid. But they did believe there were enough people stupid enough to continue buying stock and pushing the prices up, even when they were dangerously high. They believed in the "greater fool" theory, and they believed they could get out ahead of the crowd if things went pear-shaped.

The problem with the greater fool theory is that other speculators play it too. And they play it in an unpredictable environment.

The other difficulty with stock-market bubbles is that they open the door to fraudsters and other financial villains—from fee-obsessed brokers to corporate executives who artificially inflate their profits to drive their company's stock higher and higher.

Chapter 5

Basic Concepts for Investing

The journey of a thousand miles begins with one step.
– Lao Tzu

I hope that by now you are convinced that investment is the safest and most profitable strategy for generating income. I want to look at the concept of investing in more depth now. To recap, investment:

- Comes in many shapes and sizes,
- Is easy to do with a little financial education,
- Gives you control over your finances, and
- Isn't just for the super rich—you can do it too.

> WARNING: This isn't a get-rich-quick scheme. It takes time and patience, but the rewards will make it well worth the wait.

Before you invest …

Save, save, save.

Life is full of unpredictable events—a large, unexpected medical bill; job loss; and illness being just a few. To protect yourself against the tough times, you need a buffer of at least three months' salary that you can get at easily in case you need it. This should either be in ready cash (in a bank account) or in liquid assets (which are easily converted into cash).

Types of investment

Most successful investments rely on something called a **buy and hold strategy**. This means that you buy an asset, such as shares in a company, corporate or government bonds, or property, and hold onto it for a period of several years to allow its value to rise.

Investments come in many shapes and sizes, from paper assets such as bonds and stocks, to Real Estate (property), collectibles (antiques), and commodities (gold and silver).

Each of these types of investment behaves differently and each has advantages and disadvantages. In general, the higher the risk, the higher the potential return on investment. The types of investment you choose depend on the amount of risk you are able and willing to take on.

A successful investment strategy involves creating a **portfolio of assets** which react differently to particular circumstances. From this portfolio, your different assets can each earn you an income stream.

Investing to generate multiple streams of income

By creating multiple streams of income from different types of assets, you increase your number of opportunities to make money.

As we have explained, an investment is something whose value you expect to increase over time so that it exceeds the amount of money you initially put in. The profit you make thanks to this increase in value is called **return on investment**.

Income and your goals

Depending on what you want to do with your money, you may want to keep your savings where you can get at them easily. Alternatively, if you're saving up to meet a future expense, you may want to make a long-term investment that will bring higher returns.

Short-term savings

Short-term investments are usually cash or cash equivalents. The more "liquid" an asset is, the easier it is to turn your investment back into cash. A bank account is a good example of a short-term investment.

Long-term savings

If you are saving up for your child's college tuition, you can choose an investment that matures after 10 or even 20 years. The money is tied up for that period, but in exchange for its inaccessibility, the returns are higher. An example of long-term investment is a bond.

Each type of investment can earn you money in two ways:

- Capital appreciation
- Dividends

Capital appreciation is when the net value of an asset increases, whether the asset is a share, bond, property, or collector's item. Besides capital appreciation, your assets can earn you income by paying out sums of money on a regular basis. These sums are called dividends.

The following are examples of the ways different assets can earn you money:

Type of asset	Income
Deposit in a bank account	Interest paid on a monthly, quarterly, or annual basis
High-quality bonds	Guaranteed interest payments, but low rates of return
Property	Rental income, appreciation in value
Stocks / shares	Dividend payouts and (possibly) capital growth

Modern portfolio theory

In the 1950s, Harry Markowitz established a new theory called Modern Portfolio Theory. The premise of this theory is that the market is efficient; in other words, the stock market adjusts to new information so quickly that no one can accurately predict its future course.

The cornerstone of this technique is to spread risk by diversifying it across a portfolio of different assets which respond differently to different circumstances.

EXAMPLE:

To understand how this works, imagine for a moment that you have shares in two companies: a shop that manufactures umbrellas and a shop that sells sunblock.

During the winter months, the umbrella shop makes a profit and the sunblock manufacturer sustains a loss. During the summer, the positions are reversed. Both companies are risky, but in different ways.

The circumstances that negatively affect one positively affect the other, so the two are perfectly negatively correlated. By having an equal investment in both companies, you effectively offset the risks of both.

Minimizing risk by creating a portfolio

As riskier investments tend to bring higher returns, Portfolio Theory enables investors to put together different volatile stocks in such a way that the portfolio as a whole is less risky that the individual stocks.

Each type of asset has the potential to earn you money in different ways, but there's no hard and fast way to predict which assets will give you a good return on your investment. So to spread the risk and create the best possible chance of earning money, most people spread their investment over a portfolio of different assets.

An example of a portfolio might be:

An investment portfolio

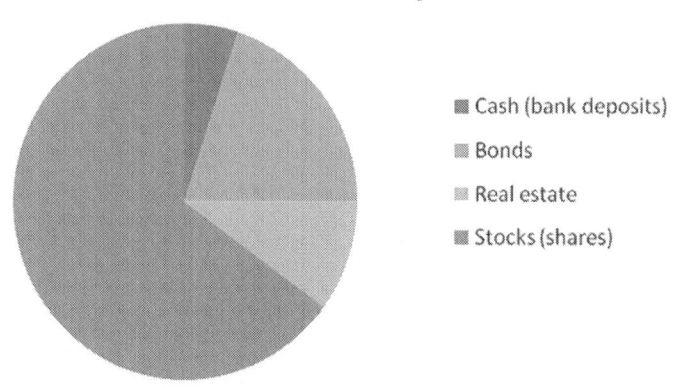

- Cash (bank deposits)
- Bonds
- Real estate
- Stocks (shares)

In a moment, we'll take a look at some of the assets you can invest in. But first, a quick word about risk and how to assess it.

Risk

> *"Twenty years from now you will be more disappointed by the things that you didn't do than by the ones you did do. So throw off the bowlines. Sail away from the safe harbor. Catch the trade winds in your sails. Explore. Dream. Discover".*
> *– Mark Twain*

In Part 1, we talked about adopting a positive attitude to help you deal with setbacks ad embrace new challenges. I want you to remember some of those lessons now as we talk about analyzing and accepting risk.

Many people put off investing in the stock market, buying bonds, or otherwise relinquishing liquid assets such as cash because they fear losing their original investment.

Risk is certainly a reality, and with some assets there is no guarantee that you will make a profit or even get back what you put in. But it's also true that doing nothing with your money is in itself a risk.

Imagine you have $100 in cash and you bury it under the floorboards for safekeeping. If you dig up that money in a year's time, it will have lost value simply because of inflation. The current rate of inflation in the United States is about 1.69%, which means that if you bury $100 today, in a year's time it will be worth only $98.31.

So you see, you can risk everything by risking nothing.

What type of investor are you?

> *Be who you are and say what you feel, because those who mind don't matter and those who matter don't mind.*
> – Dr. Seuss

Everyone is different, and your investment choices will depend as much on your personality as your goals. It's important to establish your type before making any decisions about how to invest.

The two types of investor

Roughly speaking, there are two types of investor: defensive and aggressive.

Peter

Peter's top priority is hanging onto his capital at all costs. He prefers long-term investments which require minimal effort to maintain, and which guarantee a fixed income. He prefers small, stable returns with very little risk.

Peter is a **defensive investor**.

Jane

Jane's attitude toward investing is exactly the opposite. She likes to devote time to managing her investments and knows everything about a business before investing in it. Her portfolio of stocks includes a high proportion of small, volatile companies with high growth potential.

Jane is an **aggressive investor**.

Defensive and aggressive investment game plans

Depending on what type of investor you are, different strategies might suit you best. If you fit the defensive type, sink 50% of your investment into government bonds and split the remaining 50% between diversified common stocks and investment fund shares. This spreads any risk while ensuring that a large proportion of your investment is in a steady, long-term scheme.

If you see yourself as an aggressive investor, put a third of your lump sum into government bonds, split a third between diversified common stocks and investment fund shares, and put the remaining third into timed opportunities like growth stocks, bargain issues, and companies on the brink of significant change—such as a merger, sale, or reorganization.

Quick tips for choosing an investment

Whatever type of investor you are, there are some common rules that you should consider before choosing a business to invest in.

> **Investment checklist**
> - How well is a company performing compared to its competitors?
> - What is its profit margin?
> - Has it increased or decreased its market share in recent months?

Sound investments are based on long-term, fundamental value, so when you're looking for stocks, choose companies you believe will generate wealth over time because their ongoing business operations are good, rather than companies whose shares happen to be performing well in the current market.

The same rule applies if you are investing in a mutual fund, which makes decisions about which stocks to buy on your behalf. The fund should demonstrate growth potential in the same way that individual companies might. Only buy paper assets if you can be sure the market price is below the company's actual value. That way, you'll be protected from any sudden downturns in the market.

Weighing the risk

Some assets are riskier than others. Each has advantages and disadvantages, and none of them are totally risk free. But when you find out as much as you can before you invest, you give yourself the best chance to minimize risk.

Remember the dreams you envisaged in Part 1 and the goals you set out for achieving them. Failing to act makes it impossible for you to achieve these goals. They won't happen by themselves. You have to take some risks to move forward. You have already taken a step in the right direction by beginning your financial education. Let's keep going now by finding out more about each asset type.

10 Rules to Remember

1. *A buy and hold strategy generates the best returns on average. Aim to hold your investments for the long term.*

2. *Set up multiple streams of income from different assets to maximize your earning potential.*

3. *Remember the three investment strategies: Protect your income; Earn income; Grow your money.*

4. *Make sure you have a safety net of cash savings before you invest.*

5. *Do your homework before investing in a company or mutual fund.*

6. *Match your investment strategy to your goals.*

7. *Don't put all your eggs in one basket—create a diverse portfolio to spread risk.*

8. *Decide if you are an aggressive or a defensive investor.*

9. *In 20 years, you will be more disappointed by what you didn't do that what you did.*

10. *To risk nothing is to risk everything.*

PART 3

BUILDING YOUR ASSETS

Chapter 6

An Introduction to Types of Assets

Your assets are the things that help generate income for you—either by appreciating in value or by earning income in the form of regular payments such as dividends. Each asset has its own advantages and disadvantages, and each is designed for a specific purpose.

In this chapter, we'll find out how different types of assets work.

Bank accounts

Bank accounts are one of the safest places to put your money. You are guaranteed to get back at least the amount that you deposited in the first place, and you get a monthly, quarterly, or annual return by earning interest on your savings.

Money in the bank is a **liquid asset**, which means it's equivalent to cash. This means you can get at it easily in case of an emergency, but it also means it's easy to spend accidentally.

Bank accounts at a glance

Advantages

- Your investment is guaranteed.
- You earn income in the form of interest payments on your savings.
- Your money is **liquid**, so you can get to it in case of emergency.

Disadvantages

- When interest rates are low, you will get a low return on your investment.
- Because the money is easy to access, you might be tempted to spend it.

Interest rates

Money in your account will earn interest at a certain percentage per year. This percentage is called the **interest rate,** and the interest you earn will be credited to your account monthly, quarterly, or annually, depending on your bank.

> *EXAMPLE:*
>
> *You have $100 in a bank account which offers 1.6% interest per year (1.6% AER).*
>
> *1.6% of $100 is $1.60.*
>
> *$100 + $1.60 = $101.60.*
>
> *After a year, your money will have increased to $101.60.*

Interest must keep pace with **inflation** in order for your money to retain its purchasing power. Inflation erodes your money's worth, so you need to choose a bank account that offers interest rates that are equal to or higher than inflation.

The following table demonstrates what happens when inflation is higher than interest rates.

Original investment	Interest rate	Inflation	Net worth of investment after one year
$100	1.6% AER	2%	$99.57

$100 + 1.6% = $101.60

$101.60 - 2% = $99.57

Types of bank accounts

Different bank accounts offer different interest rates. Some accounts need advance warning when you plan to withdraw your money and are designed to be long-term savings accounts. These generally offer high interest rates to compensate you for not being able to access your money immediately.

The type of account you choose will depend on the goals you set yourself in Part 1. In Part 4, we go into more detail about the types of accounts available to you, but the following is a rough guide to get you started:

Bank account	Features	Suitable for
High-interest saver account	- Often requires notice of withdrawal - High interest rates	Long-term savings plans
Retirement plans (IRAs)	- Save up to $5,000 per year	Pension plans and long-term savings
College savings funds (529)	- Individuals may contribute up to $60,000 in total, couples $120,000	Long-term savings plan for college tuition
Bank certificates of deposit (CDs)	- Original investment is insured - Fixed term (one month, three months, six months, one year) - Usually fixed interest rate	Savings plans where funds are required on a specific date; Original investment and accrued interest are withdrawn at the same time
Internet banking	- Low cost	Day-to-day savings and transactions

Bonds

Simply put, a bond is a type of IOU. If you buy a bond, you are usually advancing a loan to help fund a government scheme or a company's new venture, and you receive bonds as proof of your investment.

The **issuer** of the bond is the person or group who has borrowed money from you. You are the **creditor** (the lender). All bonds have a "**calling**" date (when they reach **maturity**), which is when the issuer must pay back the amount of money they borrowed from you.

Sources of Wealth

> **Bonds at a glance**
> - They are a good, long-term investment (5–20 years).
> - Bonds held to maturity generally do better than bonds sold early.
> - High-quality bonds guarantee regular interest payments.
> - Low-quality bonds have potentially higher returns but higher risk.

Bonds are a long-term investment and are typically held for as few as five years and as many as 20 years.

When you buy bonds, you are essentially parting with a sum of money for a substantial period of time for others to use. As a reward for this inconvenience, the bond issuer pays you interest on your initial investment, which can earn you a profit. This periodic interest payment is known as a **coupon payment.**

Coupons, yields, and prices explained

Statistically, bonds give a better rate of return if they are held to maturity. But the prices can still fluctuate on a daily basis, and bonds may be sold at any time you wish.

There are three concepts that help express these price fluctuations: **coupons, yields,** and **prices.**

COUPONS

The **coupon payment** is the periodic interest you receive between the bond being **issued** and the bond being **called** when it reaches maturity.

The **coupon rate** is the total number of coupons paid per year, divided by the bond's face value.

It is called a "coupon" because some bonds literally have coupons attached to them. Holders receive interest by stripping off the coupons and redeeming them. This is less common today as more records are kept electronically.

> EXAMPLE:
>
> If a bond has a face value of $1,000 and a coupon rate of 5%, it pays $50 per year.

YIELDS
Yield is the rate of return received from investing in a bond. There are two types:

1. Current / running yield
2. Yield to maturity / redemption yield

Current yield is the simplest version of yield and is calculated like this: *yield = coupon amount / price.* When you buy a bond at its face value, yield is equal to the interest rate. But when the price of the bond goes up or down, so does the yield.

If the price of the bond goes up, the yield must go down, and vice versa.

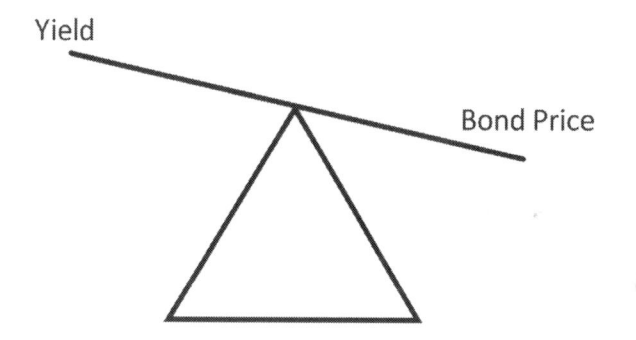

> EXAMPLE:
>
> If you buy a bond at $1,000 face value with a 10% coupon, the yield is 10% ($100/$1,000).

This is pretty simple stuff, but if the price goes down to $800, then the yield goes up to 12.5%. This happens because you are getting the same guaranteed $100 on an asset that is worth $800 ($100/$800). Conversely, if the bond goes up in price to $1,200, the yield shrinks to 8.33% ($100/$1,200).

Yield to maturity (YTM) is a more useful calculation of yield and shows the total return you will receive if the bond is held to maturity. It takes into account all the interest payments you will receive, as well as any gains (if you bought your bonds at a discount or below) or losses (if you purchased at a premium).

A **discount bond** is a bond that is issued for less than its par (or face) value or a bond currently trading for less than its par value in the secondary market.

The "discount" in a discount bond doesn't necessarily mean that investors get a better yield than the market is offering, just a price below par. Depending on the length of time until maturity, zero-coupon bonds can be issued at very large discounts to par, sometimes 50% or more.

A **premium bond** is a bond that is trading above its par value. A bond will trade at a premium when it offers a coupon rate that is higher than prevailing interest rates. This is because investors want a higher yield and will pay more for it.

> *Recommendation*
>
> *Yield to maturity is a more useful measure than current yield. It allows you to compare bonds with different coupons and maturities.*

PRICE

As we discovered earlier, when the price of a bond goes up, the yield must come down. So which is better, high prices or high yields?

That really depends on whether you are buying or selling. If you are a bond buyer, high yields mean you can buy bonds at lower prices. On a bond with a yield of 12.5% but a face value of $1,000, for example, you could purchase it at the discounted price of $800.

If you already own a bond, you want the price of the bond to go up and make you a profit.

Types of bond

Bonds come in different varieties, and each has its high and low points. High-quality bonds are low risk and will guarantee you interest payments but offer low returns. Low-quality, or "junk" bonds, have the potential to give very high returns but come with greater risk.

BONDS AT A GLANCE

Type of bond	Features
Gilt-edged bonds	High-quality, low-risk bonds offering guaranteed interest but low returns
Fixed-rate bonds	Coupon remains constant throughout the life of the bond
Floating-rate notes (FRNs)	Variable coupon linked to a reference interest rate such as LIBOR
Zero-coupon bonds (zeros)	No regular interest and issued at a substantial discount
High-yield bonds (junk bonds)	Bonds rated below investment grade by credit-rating agencies; high risk, potential high yield
Convertible bonds	Bonds that can be exchanged for shares in the issuer's common stock
Exchangeable bonds	Bonds that can be exchanged for shares in any corporation
Inflation-linked bonds (linkers)	Principal amount and interest payments indexed to inflation

Real Estate

Real Estate is one of the most secure ways to accumulate wealth and it's possible to make money whatever the market trend.

You don't actually need to have a lot of money to get started. When buying a house, for example, you contribute only a fraction of the cost and the rest is advanced by the bank, but you can still benefit from the whole value generated in terms of **cash flow** (from rent, for example) and **appreciation** (when the value of the property rises).

Why is Real Estate a good investment?

Good properties are everywhere, and it's always possible to find good deals, regardless of where you live. The trick is to buy at a low price and sell at a high one to make sure you see the full benefits of appreciation. The following are some of the benefits of investing in Real Estate:

- You don't need certification or a license to get started.
- Owning your own home forces you to start a savings program.
- Each transaction generates a substantial sum—often more than an average yearly salary.
- It's not difficult to put together a rewarding deal.
- Although you will need to take risks, it's relatively simple to evaluate these and the return on investment is generally high.
- Congress gives important tax breaks to homeowners:
    - Interest payments on mortgage and property taxes are deductible.
    - Realized gains in the value of your house are tax-exempt up to substantial amounts.
- It's possible to make a good deal regardless of whether the market is up or down:
    - If the market is up, buy, fix, or improve a property and sell it as quickly as possible.
    - If the market is following a downward trend, you can find good deals in distressed properties that can be upgraded and rented.

Where do I start?

Most people start with the residential Real Estate market before moving on to larger or commercial properties. There are three types of residential Real Estate:

- Single-family houses (require more careful assessment when you buy)
- Apartments (entry level)
- Apartment buildings (require more capital to buy and more skills to manage)

Single-family houses

Start by improving the house to increase its market value. As a general rule, a bad property in a good neighborhood is a good place to start. Once you've fixed it up, you'll be able to rent it for a higher price than the cost of the mortgage and fees.

Apartments and flats

Apartments can usually be rented for a higher price than houses, which is good news for cash flow.

Apartment buildings

These are usually bought in order to rent out to tenants. Rent payments bring in solid cash flow that you can increase by improving the apartments, reducing costs, and increasing the average number of tenants. Location plays a key part in the quality of the tenants you can expect, so choose wisely!

Getting start-up capital

For many people, the main stumbling block to buying a property is getting enough cash to make an initial purchase. Generally speaking there are three sources that can help you finance your investment:

- Institutional lenders
- Mortgage brokers
- Private lenders

Institutional lenders

These are usually banks. These lenders will approve a loan based on your credit history, the collateral you can offer, and your income capacity.

Mortgage brokers

Brokers work with several lenders to find the best solution for you. They can help you find the better mortgage deals as they work with multiple lenders. They usually apply a percentage fee on the mortgage amount.

Private lenders

These are individuals or groups that can lend you money—often friends or family.

It's possible to invest in property without putting any of your own money down. Using **Other People's Money (OPM)** gives you greater leverage because you're not relying on your own limited capital, but it can be complex to achieve. A few methods for using other people's money include using the seller as your financing source, assuming the seller's existing mortgage, or finding partners who will put money into the deal in return for a share of the revenues. These options can carry substantial risk, however, so avoid them as a first-time investor in Real Estate.

The costs of Real Estate

Buying a home comes with costs besides the down payment and mortgage payments. Different costs are assumed by the buyer or seller, depending on who benefits. Here's a breakdown of the expenses involved:

Charge description	Percentage of house value	Who pays
Title search and insurance	0.5% – 1%	Buyer
Recording fee	0.2% – 0.5%	Buyer
Legal fees	0.5% – 1%	Buyer
Real Estate transfer tax	0.01% – 2%	Seller
Real Estate broker's fee	6%	Seller

Problem

"I can't afford to buy my own property, but I would like to invest in Real Estate. What options do I have?"

Solution

Invest in Real Estate Investment Trusts (REITs). REITs are securities that work like shares on the stock exchange, but they invest in Real Estate (mortgages, for example) directly. They are great diversifiers as part of an investment portfolio.

Sifting through hundreds of individual REITs to choose which ones to invest in is a tricky business, but there are plenty of Real Estate mutual funds that will be willing to choose a portfolio of REITs on your behalf. Ownership of Real Estate gives similar rates of return to common stocks if held over a long period.

Chapter 7

Stocks and Shares

Shares are similar to bonds: When you buy a share, you are advancing money to help fund a growing company or finance a new project. Unlike bonds, however, buying a share can give you the right to have a say in how the company you've invested in is run. Shares are bought and sold on the stock market.

The Stock Market

Simply put, a market is a place where buyers and sellers can trade assets and decide on a mutually agreeable price. In the case of the stock market, those assets are shares in a company that rise or fall in value depending on the company's performance and the law of **supply and demand**.

Let's examine this a little more. If demand is high, the price of an item (in this instance, shares) will rise. If supply exceeds demand, the price will fall in order to try and shift the unwanted stock.

> EXAMPLE:
>
> A trader has 100 items, but only 90 people are interested in buying them. To encourage new buyers, the trader brings the price down. Thanks to the lower price, 20 more people want to buy the items.
>
> There are now 110 people fighting over 100 items. Demand is high, so the price of the items rises.

In the same way, the price of shares on the stock market fluctuates every day according to supply and demand. If the company is performing well and making a profit, demand increases and the value of the shares rises. As a shareholder, any dividends you receive will mirror the performance of the shares.

Primary and secondary markets

In primary markets, companies seek new funds and money flows from lenders to borrowers. In secondary markets, investors buy and sell assets that already exist among themselves. The stock market is an organized secondary market and operates a bit like a middleman between the buyers and sellers. Companies that have **"gone public"** are listed on the stock exchange and can sell their stock on the market.

Indexes

As you know, the value of individual shares changes every day. To help keep a record of these changes in valuation, certain "public" companies are listed on an index which tracks the performance of their shares from day to day.

These indexes can be found in financial publications and major papers such as *The New York Times* and the *Financial Times*.

Some key indexes

Standard & Poor's 500 Stock Index

Standard & Poor's 500 is a composite index representing the top-performing companies in the United States. It contains about three quarters of the value of all US-traded stock.

The Dow / Wilshire 5,000

This index is on a larger scale than Standard & Poor's and contains all publicly tracked US common stocks on the American and New York stock exchanges. It also covers the NASDAQ market.

Russell 3,000 and MSCI Index

The Russell 3,000 and MSCI (Morgan Stanley Capital International) list all but the very smallest stocks in the market.

Profiting from Shares

Shares can provide income in two ways: through **capital growth** (if the company you invested in grows and gains in value) and through

dividends (paid in periodic installments if the company is making a profit). You receive dividends only if the company or venture you invest in does well, so it's important to choose wisely.

Share prices have to rise in line with inflation to break even. If inflation exceeds the increase in value of your shares, you are effectively losing money.

> EXAMPLE:
>
> *If this year your shares have earned on average 2% and inflation is currently 3% per year, then you have lost 1% on your investment (2% - 3% = -1%).*

Types of shares

Much like bonds, shares come in many shapes and sizes and perform differently depending on how much risk is involved. The following is a quick snapshot of the types of stock you can buy:

Share / company description	Features
Gilt-edged securities	• Government-issued securities • Zero risk
Blue-chip shares	• Long-established companies with a track record of success • Companies usually large enough to absorb risk and hire / fire expert managers • Low, but stable returns
Preference shares	• Give shareholders the right to vote at company meetings • Shareholders entitled to dividends whether the company makes a profit or not
Shares in small growth companies	• Small companies can often expect to grow quickly, so high returns are possible. • Higher risk than blue-chip shares
Shares in emerging markets	• Emerging foreign markets have high growth potential. • Higher risk than shares issued by developed foreign countries

The benefits of owning shares

Shares are a tad more accessible to a small-time investor than other assets. Collectibles such as works of art, for example, or antiques, require a specialist's knowledge that most people do not have. Property and Real Estate, while excellent investments, do require substantial initial outlays before the profits can come in.

In the long term, the stock market has produced a better return on investment than these alternative investments. Despite economic fluctuations and rises or falls in the market, a portfolio of different shares held in the long term is likely to weather the storms and make a profit.

Some rules for investing in shares

Choose companies with a firm foundation.

Before you buy, do your research. Invest only in companies that you believe have the capacity to grow in the long term.

Don't be tempted to sell early.

Shares give their best returns when they are held for a long period. Rather than trying to anticipate whether the market will rise or fall, adopt a **buy and hold strategy**. Your shares will ride the peaks and troughs to grow in the long term.

Don't put all your eggs in one basket.

Spread your investment across different types of shares. Just as your primary investment portfolio includes diverse assets such as bonds, Real Estate, cash, and shares, make sure there is diversity across your choice of shares too.

How much does it cost to own shares?

The financial gurus estimate that $2,000 is the minimum required to invest. The reason for this is that owning shares comes with certain costs that are inversely proportional to the amount you invest, so the smaller the amount you invest, the higher the cost per share and the more a stock has to rise in order to make a decent return.

Depending on how you decide to buy your shares, the costs will vary. But you will probably have to pay something in the way of commission and management fees.

Buying shares

When it comes to buying shares, you have a number of options:

- Stockbrokers
- Internet broking
- Pooled investments

Stockbrokers

Stockbrokers generally charge a fee of $5–$20 per transaction, plus commission. Many focus on trading only, though some offer advisory and management services to help you choose a portfolio of shares and manage your investment once you've made it.

Internet broking

Thanks to Internet broking, buying shares is becoming easier and cheaper than ever before. Internet brokers can place an order on your behalf at any time and usually charge a single, flat fee of around $10 for their services. Cheap and easy? You betcha, but there are some disadvantages.

First, it's hard to get a picture of a firm's reliability that you're dealing with. Operating exclusively online means no face-to-face meetings and a limited paper trail; this can make gauging a reputation difficult.

Second, Internet brokers do not issue share certificates. This means that when you buy a share, the broker holds the title in a nominee account for you. This isn't really a problem unless you want to change brokers, which can cause a few hiccups.

Pooled investments

For the small investor, finding $2,000 to invest can be a big task. It costs even more than this to adequately diversify your stocks, putting this out of reach for many first-time investors. This is where pooled investments come in.

The idea is that a number of investors contribute to a mutual fund, which is then managed by professionals who spread the total sum across a portfolio of shares. The investors effectively buy shares in the mutual fund and benefit from its profits. The mutual fund does the diversifying, reducing the risks and making the individual's small investment go a lot farther when it's added to other people's money.

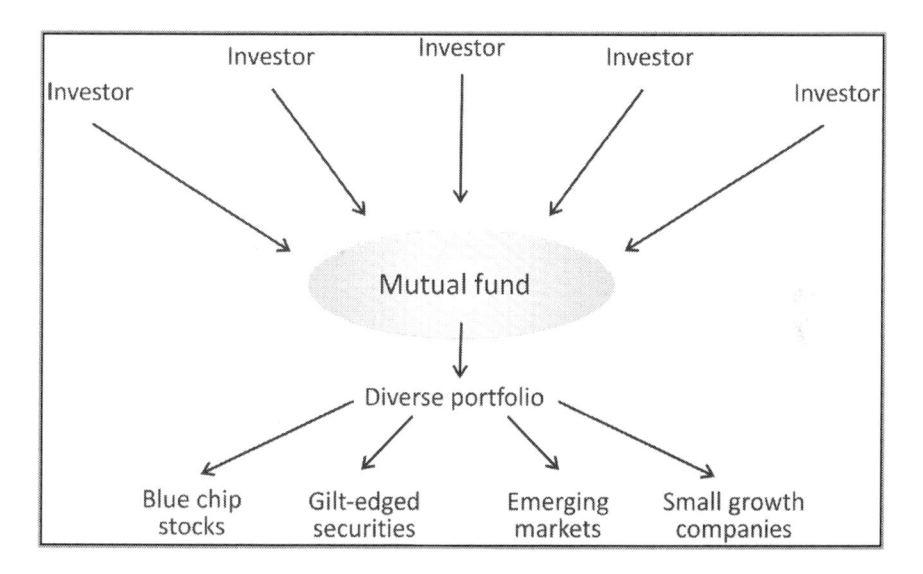

```
Investor    Investor    Investor    Investor
                                              Investor
Investor
              ↘  ↘  ↓  ↙  ↙  ↙
                 Mutual fund
                      ↓
              ┌── Diverse portfolio ──┐
             ↙      ↙       ↘         ↘
       Blue chip  Gilt-edged  Emerging  Small growth
        stocks    securities   markets   companies
```

By now, you should have a clearer picture of the types of assets available to you as an investor. The following is a quick guide to jog your memory:

Assets at a Glance

Bank accounts

- *Money in a bank account is a "liquid" asset—you can exchange it for cash whenever you want.*
- *Banks are one of the safest places to put your money.*
- *A lump sum in a bank account will earn interest.*
- *Interest must keep pace with inflation, or your money will lose purchasing power.*

Bonds

- *Bonds are a form of IOU.*
- *Bonds are a long-term investment (5–20 years).*
- *If yield goes up, prices go down (and vice versa).*
- *Different types of bonds carry different degrees of risk.*

Real Estate

- *If you have the means to own your own home, do it.*
- *Buying a property forces you to begin a regular savings program.*
- *It is possible to make money from Real Estate, whatever the market trend.*

Stocks and shares

- *The stock market works on the basis of supply and demand: When demand is high, prices rise. When it is low, prices fall.*
- *Indexes such as Standard & Poor's 500 help track the performance of shares.*
- *Profits take the form of dividends and capital gains.*
- *Different shares carry different risks.*
- *Pooling your investment (by investing in a mutual fund, for instance) can make your money go farther.*

Chapter 8

Three Investment Strategies

Now that you know a little more about the types of assets, it's time to look at which investment strategies will help you achieve your goals. The three main investment strategies are protecting your income, earning income, and growing your money. Your portfolio of assets will vary depending on which strategy you adopt, but roughly speaking, the allocation works out something like this:

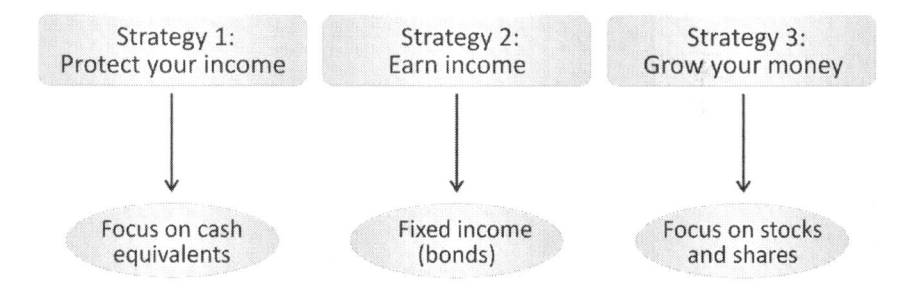

```
Strategy 1:              Strategy 2:              Strategy 3:
Protect your income      Earn income              Grow your money
       ↓                      ↓                        ↓
  Focus on cash          Fixed income            Focus on stocks
   equivalents              (bonds)                 and shares
```

Matching assets to your goals

You already know about multiple streams of income and the different assets you can choose to invest in. So now it's time to decide which are right for you. To do that you'll need to think back to the goals you set for yourself in Part 1. Different goals require different investment strategies and different asset allocations.

> *Andy and Helen's story*
>
> *Andy and Helen are a couple in their late 20s. Both are teachers, and they have a joint annual income of $70,000. They need $30,000 as a down payment for a house in one year's time.*
>
> *They have saved $25,000 already.*

Andy and Helen should use the first strategy.

Andy and Helen have a specific goal with a set deadline. As they already have some of the money they need, it is more important to protect the money that they have than to try to grow a lot more.

They should invest their money in a safe security which matures when the money is required, such as a one-year certificate of deposit (CD).

> *Wendy and Sam's story*
>
> *Wendy and Sam are a couple in their mid-30s. They have two children, ages 8 and 10. Sam works in advertising and earns $70,000 per year. Wendy is a part-time teacher with an annual income of $15,000. The couple would like to see both children go to college.*
>
> *The couple own their own house and Sam has shares worth $10,000 in his company. They have $10,000 in savings.*

Wendy and Sam should use a combination of the second and third strategies.

For Wendy and Sam, growing their money is the goal. They are both young enough to be able to weather the ups and downs of the future and have enough earning potential to be able to risk more volatile investments. As their children are young, they have almost 10 years to raise the money they need before college fees are due.

They should choose an investment vehicle tailored to their goal of saving for the purpose of their children's education. For this goal, a 529 savings account is an appropriate vehicle. This particular savings account allows parents and grandparents to give gifts to children for the purpose of a college education. Individuals can contribute up to $60,000 and couples can contribute up to $120,000. Savings in these accounts are exempt from federal taxes as long as the earnings are used for college education.

A feature of the 529 savings account is that income can be reinvested in stocks and bonds. For Wendy and Sam, it makes sense to reinvest interest earned on their savings in a portfolio of shares, which will each contribute a stream of income that can be cashed in in stages or reinvested until the money is needed for college fees in a few years.

In Part 4, we'll go into detail about how to allocate your assets according to your goals and the type of investor you are. But for now, let's spend some time thinking about the role your personality can have on your decisions.

Chapter 9

Paying Tax on Your Assets

Besides graduated income tax, any profits you make on investments such as stocks and shares will be subject to tax. There are exceptions, and some investment programs and savings accounts are designed to allow your investments to grow tax free (we discuss these in Part 4), but in most cases you'll be liable for two types of taxation: **dividends tax** and **capital gains tax**.

Dividends tax

Simply put, dividends are periodic distributions of profit, or pay-outs, received from a corporation, trust, estate, or partnership. Most commonly, dividends are received as profit on shares owned in a particular company.

> *Warning: If you receive dividends on your shares and reinvest these in the stock market, they still count as taxable dividends and you need to declare them on your tax return.*

Capital gains tax

Capital gains tax is in essence a sales tax levied on capital assets. Capital assets include almost everything an individual owns, whether for investment purposes or simply for personal use and enjoyment. Your home, car, household furnishings, jewelry, and stocks and bonds all count as capital assets in the eyes of the tax man.

If you sell these assets and realize a profit from that sale, you are required to pay capital gains tax. Generally, this type of tax is most often seen on property sales, but it also applies to some types of trade. When you redeem (sell) stocks, for instance, you are liable for capital gains tax. The same applies to bonds that have reached their maturity.

> ## Recommendation
>
> *The tax system is complex and distinctions among different types of taxation can be thorny. If you're not sure what you should be paying, it's always worth seeking the advice of a professional to guide you through these murky waters. They may be able to point out tax breaks too.*

Paying capital gains and dividends tax

When you pay tax on your regular income or salary, it is usually deducted from your paycheck before you see the money. This method of automatic tax deduction is called "**withholding**" tax.

Capital gains and dividends tax work slightly differently. They are recorded by filing a tax return with the IRS. It's worth taking a look at the IRS website (http://www.irs.gov/) to find out exactly what's required. They'll also be able to help with tax questions and provide all the forms you need to complete your tax return.

Chapter 10

Financial Advisors

Making an investment can be a daunting prospect—particularly for first-timers. So how do you get the information you need to make an informed decision about where to invest your money? And whose advice can you trust?

Well, the short answer is that no one can give you the right answers. Ultimately, you have to trust your own judgment and do your own research. Some professional advisors have an agenda of some sort, whether it's charging a hefty fee for their services or reaping a slice of your profits. Even without the complication of an agenda, there's a limit to the usefulness of any technique, however sophisticated, that aims to predict the market.

Meanwhile, the people you trust—family and friends—may have excellent intentions but won't necessarily know more than you do about investing. If they do have investment experience, it's likely to be very specific and largely irrelevant to your particular situation.

It's important not to assume that everyone else knows more about this than you do. They may be repeating hints heard from someone else, or they may have gotten lucky on the off-chance.

Types of financial advisors

Seeking professional advice does have its advantages. When it comes to taxes, it's often absolutely necessary. Professional advisors are also required to have proper certification and insurance, which offers you some level of protection if things go wrong. On the flipside, their services can be costly and your investments will need to perform very well to offset management fees and commission.

Let's meet some of the key players:

- Professional investment advisors

- Financial services firms
- Brokerage houses

Professional investment advisors usually aim to preserve your wealth and offer the advantage of years of experience that can help protect you from costly mistakes. The flipside is that they tend to charge substantial annual fees in return for advice and management.

Financial services firms are good providers of regular bulletins reflecting how the market is behaving. Usually they suggest buying or selling based on short-term forecasts of market trends regardless of current price—forecasts which are supposedly worked out using "advanced technical methods" that are often left unexplained. It's not possible to tell how these firms reach their conclusions because that information is proprietary, which means it can be difficult to decide how far to trust the information. However, they can be a useful starting point from which to begin your own analysis.

Brokerage houses act as an intermediary between buyers and sellers and provide a lot of free information. They work on commission, which means they are likely to encourage you to buy or sell, and are closely aligned with day-to-day market trends, so their information is more useful for speculation than investment.

FINANCIAL ADVISORS AT A GLANCE

Type of advisor	What they can help with
Accountants	Tax
Actuaries	Insurance / pension transfers
Company representatives	Company (including bank) finance products, i.e., bank accounts, savings plans, and mortgages
IFAs	Comparison of financial products from different companies
Attorneys	Wills and probate
Stockbrokers	Stocks and shares

Everyone should be prepared to seek advice when they need it, and it's often a vital part of your financial education too. But while many experts can benefit you, there have been occasions when even the best and brightest have gotten it wrong. In Part 4, we'll discover how.

5 Rules to Remember

1. Profits made on your investments are taxable—either by capital gains or dividends tax.

2. When in doubt about how much tax to pay, seek professional advice.

3. Don't assume that everyone else knows more about investing than you do...

4. ...but don't be afraid to seek professional advice when you need it.

5. Make sure you are aware of all fees and commission charges before you commit to working with a financial advisor

PART 4

"IT'S COMPLICATED" – TECHNIQUES THE PROS USE

Whether you think you can or think you can't, you're right.

– Henry Ford

Following years of relative stability in the markets, the financial industry in the United States experienced significant growth between 2001 and 2007. Part of this growth was thanks to the booming Real Estate market. Mortgage lenders such as Fannie May and Freddie Mac were offering mortgages with almost zero down payments. The result was an unprecedented housing boom as people who had previously been unable to afford their own homes were suddenly able to purchase.

The resulting creation of substantial unsecured debt was bundled together with other loans by investment banks and sold on to investors as a security called CDOs—Collateralized Debt Obligations. These CDOs were extremely volatile because there was no guarantee the original borrowers could pay back their loans, but they were represented as fail-safe securities by the banks that sold them and given the highest possible rating by the ratings agencies: AAA.

Reassured by the high ratings, investors purchased CDOs by the truckload, even while the investment banks who sold them were betting against these securities in the expectation that the homeowners would default on their loans.

In 2008, that's exactly what happened. The many who were unable to pay the mortgages they should never have been offered in the first place defaulted on their loans. Foreclosures were numerous, and as the loans went bad, the lenders who had offered them failed. The market for CDOs collapsed, leaving investors bereft and the investment banks floundering.

On September 15, financial giants Lehman Brothers filed for bankruptcy. On the same day, Bank of America announced its intention to buy Merrill Lynch & Co. for $50 billion. Later that month, the federal government took over American International Group (AIG), costing tax payers $150 billion.

The rest, as they say, is history. The financial crisis led to one of the largest recessions of the last two centuries. Unemployment reached new heights and the world in 2012 was still feeling the consequences of a shaken economy. So what went so wrong? Where did the experts fail, and why did no one see this coming?

Where the experts failed

The bankers who helped cause the financial crisis by trading in unsecured debts did so because of the conflict between making money for themselves and their companies, and making money for their investors.

By selling volatile CDOs but betting against them, the financial leaders of the big banks were able to make billions of dollars of capital for themselves—but they could achieve this success only by disguising bad loans as solid investments.

Of course, the bankers could not admit to this duplicity after the recession took place. It would undermine their authority, their expertise, and their right to the capital they had dubiously earned.

The ratings agencies that had awarded AAA grades to CDOs declined to accept responsibility, saying their ratings were merely "opinion" and not designed to form the basis of any investment decision.

Meanwhile, the bankers themselves blamed their faulty recommendations to investors to buy CDOs on the complexity of the systems they used. The excuse ringing round the courtrooms was that the systems used to predict the markets, regulate investments, and judge risk were too complicated to allow for simplistic judgments.

In this situation, the experts let us down. It is true that the systems are complex. But they are not too complicated to be understood by people like you and me. Despite increased regulation in the financial industry, conflict of interest remains a factor in banking today and many of the men and women instrumental in bringing the financial sector to its knees still have considerable influence in the financial world.

You can't always tell who to trust and who to avoid. Many of the professionals in the financial services realm are credible, honest, and capable men and women. You can't always get a reliable picture of who are the goodies and the baddies. But you can understand the systems that the professionals use to advise you on your investments. You can become as adept as they are. You can protect yourself from becoming the victims of private greed by educating yourself. And in this part of the book, I'm going to show you how.

Chapter 11

Basic Principles

Do not worry if you have built your castles in the air. They are where they should be. Now put the foundations under them.
— Henry David Thoreau

The job of financial professionals is to judge which assets in the stock market will produce the best rates of return for investors. This requires financiers and analysts to be able to decide how much a particular asset is worth and to try to predict its course in the stock market.

Broadly speaking, financial professionals use two techniques for evaluating the worth of stocks and shares, which Burton G. Malkiel calls "firm foundation theory" and "castle-in-the-air theory."

Firm foundation theory

According to firm foundation theory, each investment, whether paper assets or Real Estate, has an **intrinsic value**. To make a profit on your investment, you need to wait until the market value falls below this base line and then take the opportunity to buy up assets at these low prices, confident they will rise at least as high as their true market value.

Determining intrinsic value

There's no hard-and-fast rule to accurately determine an asset's intrinsic value. But certain indicators are useful to help you judge current success:

- Stream of earnings
- Performance of the company compared to its peers in the same industry
- Profit margin (compared to peers)
- Who's on the staff
- Growth expectation
- Past performance

There's nothing wrong with these indicators per se, but they do need a couple of caveats. Firstly, past performance, while it may demonstrate a commendable track record, is no guarantee of future success. Secondly, a staff of excellent professionals headed by a competent boss is certainly a good sign, but there's no guarantee that these people won't move to another company, taking their worth with them.

Castle-in-the-air theory

Castle-in-the-air theory relies on anticipating which stocks are likely to produce the most excitement among potential investors. As we saw in Part 2, excitement is catching and public fervor over a particular investment can quickly establish a crowd following.

In castle-in-the-air theory, successful investors try to beat the crowds by identifying situations that are susceptible to whipping up public expectation. Then they buy early, leaving the investors who follow in their wake to push stock prices higher and higher.

If castle-in-the-air theory is successful, the result is bubbles which grow and grow until they burst, pushing stocks to extraordinary heights before the market turns and investors quickly lose money. This sort of investment is exceptionally risky for the reasons that we investigated in the second part of this book. But let's remind ourselves again why speculation of this sort is a bad idea:

1. The risks are high. You could make a lot of money, but it is just as easy to lose the lot.
2. Speculation relies on predicting which way the market will go. It is almost impossible to do this reliably enough to be sure of getting a return on your investment.
3. You have to be in the right place at the right time. Woe to the day trader who's on holiday when the market begins to turn.
4. There's no easy exit strategy.

Building castles in the air means that you are always relying on someone being stupider than you are. The problem with this "greater fool" theory is that other investors are relying on it too. Sooner or later, someone has to be the greatest fool. There's no guarantee that it won't be you.

> *Recommendation*
>
> Do not base your investment decisions on castles in the air unless you can afford to lose the money.

Chapter 12

Predicting the Future

Whether or not they prefer firm foundation or castle-in-the-air theory, the job of most professional financiers and analysts is to accurately predict the future course of stock prices, and therefore decide on the most appropriate time to buy and sell assets in order to make a profit. The two theories we have just introduced are the most popular, but they certainly aren't the only techniques in the business.

Foolish prediction techniques

While some techniques at least have a foundation in common sense, there are plenty that do not. In the late 1960s, for example, Ira Cobleigh put forward a technique called "The Hemline Indicator," which attempted to draw parallels between stock prices and the hemlines of women's skirts and dresses—the shorter the skirts, the higher the stock prices; the longer the skirts, the lower the prices.

As you can imagine, this theory was about as accurate as a blind javelin thrower, but it wasn't the last of its kind, and at one point it had a large following. Another once-popular theory was called the Super Bowl Indicator (which forecasted how the market would perform depending on who won the Super Bowl).

If nothing else, examples like these serve as a warning to us all to take methods of predicting the stock market with at least a pinch of salt.

More sensible techniques

Among the more sensible techniques advanced by Wall Street professionals are **Technical Analysis** and **Fundamental Analysis**. These are two of the biggest players in the financial services today.

Technical Analysis

Technical analysis is the prediction method favored by those professionals who take castle-in-the-air theory as the cornerstone of their analysis. These analysts are called **chartists.**

Fundamental Analysis

Fundamental analysis is the tool of choice for those who use firm foundation theory. They believe that by estimating a security's potential future growth, they can estimate its **intrinsic value.**

How technical analysis works

The pros who use technical analysis are **chartists**, by and large. As the name suggests, a chartist makes charts which track the movement of individual stock prices in order to establish trends and predict future movements.

Chartists believe that all of the information one might need about company earnings, dividends, and future performance is reflected in the market's valuation of that particular stock. As a result they use only the previous market prices to plot their charts.

The following is an example of a chart tracking stock prices:

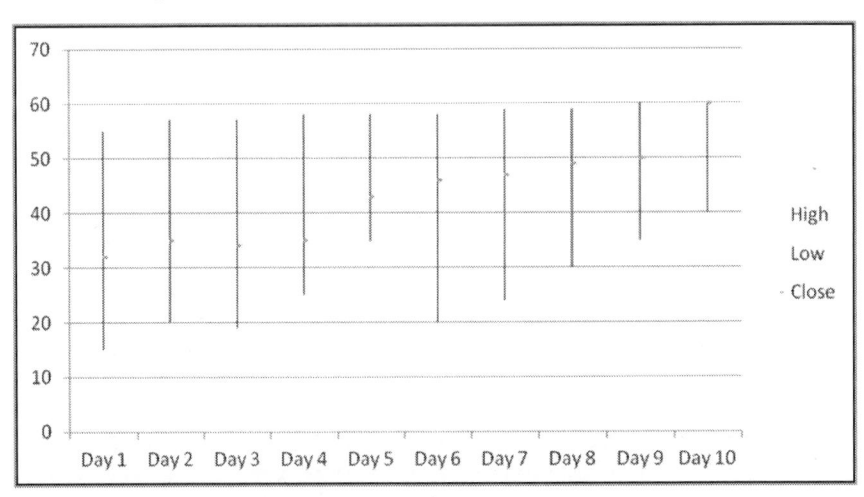

As we know, stock prices fluctuate during the course of a day, and the chart takes this into account. The top of the vertical line reflects the stock's highest selling point in that particular day, and the bottom reflects the lowest selling point. The small horizontal line that intersects the vertical is the level the stock reached at the day's close.

This chart depicts a rising trend in stock prices. A chartist might interpret this as a continuing upwards trend and make a recommendation to buy this particular stock in expectation of further increases in the price in the future.

The pros and cons of charting

There is an advantage to charting, which is that investors who see a rising trend may jump on the bandwagon and push stock prices higher thanks to new demand. This has the consequence of confirming the chartist's predictions about the existence of a rising trend, which becomes a self-fulfilling prophecy.

However, there are disadvantages to this method too. In the first instance, the chartist makes a recommendation to buy or sell based on a trend that has already been established. By the time he acts on this information, it may be too late and another trend may have begun. Another downside is that once a technique has been proven to be successful, more and more people use it. As a result, its usefulness declines as the element of exclusive knowledge vanishes.

Finally, we should question whether the "trends" we are seeing are actually trends at all. Even random occurrences can look like trends when plotted on a graph. For example, imagine flipping a coin which lands on heads five times in a row. There seems to be a pattern of success for heads, but in reality the chances of getting heads are still 50/50. The pattern is just an illusion.

Ultimately, the stock market is random. Trends may be seen to establish themselves, but overall, in the long run, the market will correct itself to maintain some sort of equilibrium. In general, what goes up must come down, and vice versa. If the market as a whole is demonstrating a sharp upward trend, that trend must and will be reversed at some point.

Fundamental Analysis

Fundamental analysts try to establish a stock's intrinsic value using four basic determinants:

1. Expected growth rate
2. Expected dividend payout
3. Risk
4. Market interest rates

Assigning a monetary value to these criteria is tricky because there are no boundaries to the data you select as the basis of your analysis. This means your figures will vary depending on whether you look at growth rate (for example) over a period of one, two, or five years.

> EXAMPLE:
>
> Imagine you have a business which sells oranges. In the first year you sell 100 oranges. In the second year, you sell 110. Your company has grown by 10%. In order to continue growing at 10%, you will have to sell a higher number of oranges each year. You can't just sell ten more next year and still grow by 10%.
>
> Here's what would happen to your company if it were to grow by 10% each year:

Year	Oranges sold	Increase on number of oranges sold last year	Percentage growth
1	100	N/A	N/A
2	110	10	10%
3	121	11	10%
4	133	12	10%

By the fourth year, you have to sell 12 oranges instead of 10 to match your 10% yearly growth rate. As time goes on, these numbers rapidly increase.

In the same way, if a company estimates 5% growth rate, this may not be achievable in real terms in the long run.

Imagine you want to invest in a company, but only if it demonstrates a healthy rate of growth over a long period. How do you determine what this is? What counts as significant growth: 5%? 10%? 15%? And what constitutes a "long period": Five years? 10? 15?

Depending on the percentages and time periods you choose, the calculations you will have to make will be very different. The data you are using are undetermined, which means it's impossible to get any precise figures from an analysis like this.

Similar problems assert themselves for the other determinants of asset value. Expected dividend payout is closely linked to company growth, for example. If a company only pays dividends when it is making a profit, it follows that these dividends will closely follow the company's growth trend.

Risk is a little different and is judged according to two types: systematic and unsystematic risk.

Systematic risk is the tendency of stocks to follow the market as a whole and reflects the variable nature of stock prices in general. This type of risk carries potentially high rewards as risky stocks often have high growth potential.

Systematic risk is assigned a value called "**beta**." A beta of 1 relates to the broad market index as measured by the S&P 500. If a stock has a beta of 2, it will swing twice as far as the market, so if the market rises by 10%, the stock can be expected to rise by 20%, and vice versa.

Unsystematic risk is unrelated to the market as a whole and refers to risk factors particular to a company—personnel changes, new product launches, and approaching mergers or takeovers, for example. Unlike systematic risk, there is no reward for investing in stocks with high unsystematic risk.

How to use fundamental analysis

If you are going to use fundamental analysis, look for stock at low prices which has high growth potential. This means that if the company does grow according to your expectations, that's a bonus for you. If it doesn't, then at least you bought the stock at a discount (i.e., below what you judge to be its intrinsic value) and haven't lost money.

You can also cash in on other people's expectations by buying stock with a firm foundation value, but which also has an inspiring story attached on which other investors can start building castles in the air.

A final word

You are now up to speed on some of the techniques financial professionals use to help judge which assets to buy and which to sell. Of course, the farther you drill down into these techniques, the more complex and sophisticated they become. We have only scratched the surface here, but this level of understanding is enough to help you see the flaws in systems which attempt to predict the market.

The experts do not always get it right. Do seek their advice, but don't be afraid to trust your own judgment in the end.

3 Rules to Remember

1. The experts don't always get it right.
2. Sometimes there is a conflict of interest between what is good for investors and what will make money for the financial advisors themselves.
3. Financial professionals aim to judge which assets will produce the highest returns using two techniques:

    a) Firm foundation theory

    b) Castle-in-the-air theory

Firm foundation theory	Castle-in-the-air theory

- Holds that each asset has a fundamental value
- Uses fundamental analysis to determine that value, using four determinants:
    o Growth rate
    o Dividend pay-out
    o Risk
    o Market interest rates
- The flaw in this theory is that it's difficult to assign monetary values to unspecific data which relies on future predictions
	- Aims to predict which stocks will whip up public excitement because they have a good story behind them
	- Uses technical analysis to determine value by creating charts which show market trends
	- Unfortunately, random events such as flipping a coin can look like patterns when drawn on a graph.

PART 5

A PRACTICAL GUIDE FOR INVESTORS

*In any situation, the best thing you can do is the right thing;
the next best thing you can do is the wrong thing;
the worst thing you can do is nothing.*

– Theodore Roosevelt

By now you've come a long way on your journey to becoming a successful investor. You're familiar with the basic concepts of finance and investment and you've come across some of the sophisticated techniques the financial professionals use.

Part 5 is a do-it-yourself guide useful to all investors, whatever your age, lifestyle, or goals. In this section, I offer specific advice tailored to different investment goals and suitable for people at specific stages in their lives.

In this chapter you will learn:

- ✓ How to assess your ability to absorb risk
- ✓ How to protect yourself from the unexpected
- ✓ Which investment strategies offer the best long-term returns
- ✓ How you can achieve your goals
- ✓ What investments are right for your life stage

Getting into practice

By now, you know that the market as a whole moves randomly and is impossible to predict accurately. But just because the market moves randomly doesn't mean individual stocks do, and you shouldn't either. The advice offered in this chapter is to help you make sensible investment decisions that will bring decent returns and help you weather the storms of a turbulent and unpredictable market.

Chapter 13

Before You Invest ...

In the second part of this book we examined the two types of investor: aggressive and defensive. Aggressive investors balance their portfolio in favor of slightly riskier investments that have faster growth potential than more stable investments such as blue-chip shares.

I want to come back to this idea in relation to risk. Where risk is concerned, two factors come into play:

1. Your attitude toward risk
2. Your ability to absorb risk

The first factor deals entirely with your personality. If you're a bit of a daredevil, you may relish uncertainty and the possibilities that come with it. If you're more cautious by nature, you may prefer to take fewer risks in return for potentially lower returns on your investment.

You need to find a balance between both factors. You wouldn't jump out of a plane without a parachute simply because you're a fan of the adrenaline rush. The same idea applies to investing—feeling happy with taking risks doesn't mean you are practically able to deal with the consequences when things go wrong. You need to find a happy medium.

Assessing your ability to handle risk

How much risk you can take on depends on several factors:

- Your age (and the number of years you have left to earn money)
- Your existing assets (Do you own your own house, for example?)
- Your earning potential (the industry you work in and the salary you can expect to make)
- Whether or not you have any dependents (such as young children)

> *Meet Mary*
>
> *Mary is 55 years old. Her health is poor, which makes it impossible for her to work. She is recently widowed and has a small income thanks to her deceased husband's life insurance policy.*

Mary's ill health means that her earning potential is nonexistent and she no longer has the support of a partner's income. She is not in a position to take on high-risk investments.

> *Meet Lucy*
>
> *Lucy is 30 years old. She is single and has no children. She has a successful career as a lawyer in the city and recently bought her first apartment.*

For Lucy, things are very different. At 30 years old she is young enough to have a considerable period of her working life ahead of her, and she is in a job with high earning potential. With no children, she has no dependents relying on her. Lucy's position means that she will be able to ride out downward trends in the market.

Build your safety net

> *Don't let life discourage you; everyone who got where he is had to begin where he was.*
> *– Richard L. Evans*

Now that you understand what risks you can take on, it's time to build your safety net. This is vital if you're going to have financial security. Your safety net will look a bit like this:

```
                    Safety net
                   /          \
           Cash reserves     Insurance
```

Cash reserves

Burton G. Malkiel, whose excellent book *A Random Walk Down Wall Street* is a must-read for any would-be investor, offers these words of advice:

> The single most important thing you can do to achieve financial security is to begin a regular savings program and to start it as early as possible.

Why save?

Saving gives you a cushion for the tough times and should be in liquid form (in a high-interest bank account, for example) so that you can get at it instantly in an emergency.

> **RULE NUMBER 1:** Work toward having liquid savings worth at least three months' salary in case of an emergency like sudden unemployment or a large medical bill.

Problem

"I can't possibly save enough money to give me financial security. My earnings are too low and I don't know where to begin."

Solution

Start a regular savings plan where you aim to put money aside each week. Even small amounts can quickly grow thanks to compound interest.

For many people, low earnings are a reality. But not having many assets to start with doesn't mean that you can't still gain financial security and start an exciting program of investment.

A program of regular saving—and by that I mean saving every week—can produce substantial amounts of money given enough time. Even if you can afford to set aside only $20 per week, or $15, or even $10—your money will still grow with time, thanks to something called **compound interest.** Compound interest basically means that the interest you earned on an investment can be reinvested to earn yet more interest. Your money starts to grow by itself.

Let me show you what I mean. The following table shows what happens to an investment of $100 per month, invested in a bank account which earns 5% interest.

Year	Yearly investment	Total deposit	Annual income (5% interest)	Cumulative income	Total value
1	$1,200	$1,200	$60	$60	$1,260
2	$1,200	$2,400	$123	$183	$2,583
3	$1,200	$3,600	$186	$372.15	$3,972.15
4	$1,200	$4,800	$258.61	$630.76	$5,430.76
5	$1,200	$6,000	$331.54	$962.30	$6962.30

Net investment compared to investment with cumulative interest

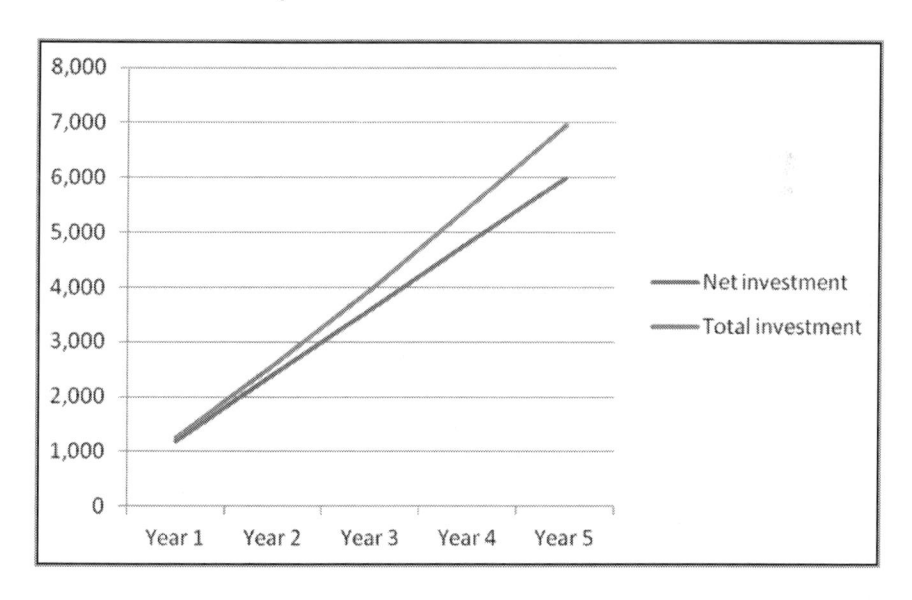

After five years, you have earned $962.30 on your original investment just through earning interest. After ten years, your cumulative deposits of $12,000 will be worth $15,848.14.

Beating inflation

Problem

"I need cash reserves for emergencies, but inflation is higher than the interest I earn in my savings account. How can I build up my liquid assets without losing purchasing power?"

Solution

Investigate short-term liquid investments that are liquid but protected from inflation. Some examples are mutual funds, bank Certificates of Deposit (CDs), and Treasury Bills.

Money-market mutual funds

Mutual funds are open-ended funds that invest in short-term, low-risk securities. They are generally regarded as being one of the safest instruments for protecting and growing your cash reserves and offer higher yields than bank deposits.

Advantages	Disadvantages
- Interest rates are relatively high, varying between 2-5%. - Low-risk investment - Yields are higher than bank deposits.	- Some mutual funds charge management fees and other expenses.

Tax exempt money-market funds

These funds invest in short-term, high-quality state issues and perform best for people in a high tax bracket. The yields on a tax-exempt fund are lower than on taxable funds, but the difference is offset because you do not have to pay a hefty tax bill on the income you do make.

Bank Certificates of Deposit (CDs)

CDs can be bought with different maturity dates depending on when you anticipate needing to access the funds you have saved. For example, if a school fees bill is due in two years' time, you can buy a CD which will mature in time to meet the bill.

Advantages	Disadvantages
- Varying maturities, generally of one, two, or three years - Government insured up to $100,000	- CDs are not easily converted into cash and there are penalties for withdrawing your money before the CDs mature. - Yield is subject to tax.

Treasury Bills (T-Bills)

Advantages	Disadvantages
- Safe, liquid investment - Issued and guaranteed by the US government - Varying maturities (4 weeks, 6 months, 1 year, etc.) - Income is exempt from state and local taxes.	- Minimum $1,000 face value

Insurance

> *By failing to prepare, you are preparing to fail.*
> – Benjamin Franklin

Besides cash reserves, the other protective measure you need is insurance. Insurance is vital. I cannot stress this enough, so I am going to say it again:

INSURANCE IS VITAL.

Insurance protects you from the unexpected. If you can't afford to replace everything you own, you'll need insurance to protect your assets—your home, your possessions, your car, and yourself.

Let's look at it this way. Imagine you are taken ill one day. You complain of headaches and are referred to the hospital for an MRI scan. When the results come through, you are told that you need a lifesaving operation. The cost of an MRI scan alone is over $1,000. Add that to consultation fees and the operation itself, and the costs mount very high very quickly.

Even if you have diligently saved to give yourself a cash buffer worth three months' income, a single unlucky event could make a serious dent in your emergency stash.

In many cases, your employer will offer health / disability insurance as part of your benefits package. You may also want to investigate home insurance and auto insurance.

Life insurance

If you have young children who are dependent on you, it makes sense to investigate taking out a life insurance policy to provide for your loved ones if you die. These come in two basic types: high premium and low premium.

High-premium policies

High-premium accounts combine insurance with an investment account (savings plan). This means that you can build up cash value as you pay money into your policy, as well as guaranteeing that the people you leave behind will receive death benefits.

You are billed regularly for a policy like this, which means that saving becomes obligatory, and any earnings you receive are tax free. The flipside is that premiums like this often come with hefty sales charges.

Low-premium policies

Low-premium policies offer death benefits only, with no buildup of cash value.

Choosing the right insurance plan

Life insurance is a must for many people. But how do you go about choosing the right plan? As you get older, your priorities will change, which should be reflected in your policy. For example, if you are a father to two young children, you need a policy which offers high levels of protection. As the children get older and more independent, the need for protection diminishes.

In this situation, it makes sense to invest in a plan which alters to reflect your needs as you get older. Policies like these are called **renewable term insurance** and allow you to renew your policy without undergoing a physical examination. You can also get something called **decreasing term insurance**, which allows you to renew your policy for progressively smaller amounts.

10 Rules to Remember

1. Your attitude toward risk and your ability to absorb risk may not be the same thing.
2. Your attitude toward risk depends on your personality: Are you a risk taker by nature, or do you carefully weigh up the pros and cons?
3. How much risk you can absorb depends on your age, earning potential, existing assets, and whether you have anyone who is dependent on you.
4. Before you invest, you need to build a safety net of cash reserves and insurance.
5. Saving regularly is the single-best thing you can do to build financial security.
6. Even a very small amount of money can grow quickly thanks to compound interest.
7. To beat inflation, investigate short-term liquid investment vehicles such as money-market funds, T-Bills, and CDs.
8. If you can't afford to replace everything you own, you need insurance.
9. Life insurance is available as a high-premium or low-premium policy.
10. Decreasing term insurance allows you to automatically renew your policy for smaller and smaller amounts as your need for protection diminishes.

Chapter 14

Choosing Your Assets

It is often said that the way you choose to invest depends on whether you want to eat well or sleep well. If you want to eat well, your portfolio of investments will be more heavily weighted toward riskier assets with high potential returns. If you want to sleep well, you'll go for the safer options and long-term strategies.

Later in the chapter we'll take another look at putting together a portfolio of assets. Whether you prefer to eat or sleep well, it's still important that you diversify your investments to offset risk as much as possible.

In the meantime, the following is a brief guide to the type of risk you can expect from various assets.

Assets according to risk

Type of asset	Estimated rates of return (%)	Risk
Bank accounts	1 – 3.5	No risk of losing your investment
Bank Certificates of Deposit	1 – 4	No risk of losing your investment
Money-market funds	3 – 5	Low risk, though funds are not usually guaranteed
Treasury Bills (T-Bills)	2.5 (+ inflation rate)	Low risk if held to maturity
High-quality corporate bonds	6	Low risk if held to maturity
Portfolio of blue-chip stocks	7 – 8	Moderate risk; Losing value on your original investment is possible.
Real Estate	7 – 8	Moderate risk
Portfolio of small-growth company stocks	8 – 9	High risk; It's not uncommon to lose 50% of stock value.
Portfolio of stocks from emerging markets	8 – 9	High risk; Market value fluctuations up or down 50% are common.

Chapter 15

Building Your Investment Portfolio

In Part 2 we looked at the advantages of earning multiple streams of income. It's now time to think about how to split your investment across these different sorts of assets. This allocation will be slightly different for everyone, depending on your age, capacity for risk, and lifestyle.

Example portfolios for each age group

The following are some examples of template portfolios for each age group. These are intended only to be examples for guidance—you may want to allocate your assets in a different way, and of course that's absolutely fine. But these figures will give you a starting point to make your own informed decisions about what to do with your money.

20s

Asset class	Percentage	Explanation
Cash	5%	Split this allocation between bank deposits and money-market funds with a midterm maturity.
Bonds	20%	Zero coupon bonds, high-quality bonds, small percentage of junk bonds
Stocks	65%	Two thirds in high-quality US stocks, one third in emerging markets
Real Estate	10%	Portfolio of REITs

Analysis

Those in their 20s with a steady stream of income have a fairly high capacity for risk. They have youth on their side, which means plenty of time to earn income and ride out the peaks and troughs of the market.

30s / 40s

Asset class	Percentage	Explanation
Cash	5%	Split this allocation between bank deposits and money-market funds with a midterm maturity.
Bonds	25%	Zero coupon bonds, high-quality bonds, small percentage of junk bonds
Stocks	60%	Two thirds in high-quality US stocks, one third in emerging markets
Real Estate	10%	Portfolio of REITs

Analysis

For couples without children, the capacity for risk is still fairly high. Those with children may be anticipating college fees and will need to tread more carefully in order to save adequately.

50s

Asset class	Percentage	Explanation
Cash	5%	Split this allocation between bank deposits and money-market funds with a midterm maturity.
Bonds	35%	Zero coupon bonds, high-quality bonds
Stocks	50%	Two thirds in high-quality US stocks, one third in emerging markets
Real Estate	15%	Portfolio of REITs

Analysis

If you're in this group, you'll need to start thinking about planning for retirement, whatever your other goals. The asset allocation is more heavily weighted toward dependable securities such as high-quality bonds with guaranteed returns.

60s

Asset class	Percentage	Explanation
Cash	10%	Split this allocation between bank deposits and money-market funds with a midterm maturity.
Bonds	40%	Zero coupon bonds, high-quality bonds
Stocks	35%	Two thirds in high-quality US stocks, one third in emerging markets
Real Estate	15%	Portfolio of REITs

Analysis

Those in their 60s and 70s will hopefully be lucky enough to enjoy their retirement. At this stage, protection against potentially large health costs becomes a priority, and capacity for risk diminishes.

Rebalancing your portfolio

You should now have an idea of what sort of investment portfolio is right for you. As we talked about in Part 2, part of the way you shape your portfolio depends on whether you are an aggressive or defensive investor.

You might remember these basic asset allocations:

Defensive investor: 50% government bonds, 50% common stocks

Aggressive investor: 33% government bonds, 33% common stocks, 33% timed opportunities (growth stocks and bargain issues)

Try to match up these allocations with the ones estimated for your age group and life stage to find a balance that suits you.

Once you decide on your allocations, you need to keep an eye on them every now and then to check that the proportions still hold.

Here's what I mean:

> *EXAMPLE:*
>
> *You decide that your portfolio should include 50% bonds and 50% stocks. You divide your funds up into these proportions.*
>
> *A year later, your stocks have risen dramatically, but bonds have fallen. The proportions have altered with the value of your assets, and your portfolio is now 60% stocks and 40% bonds.*
>
> *You decide that 60-40 is too risky. To reset the original balance, you sell some of your stocks and buy more bonds to bring it back to 50-50.*
>
> *Rebalancing your portfolio allows you to keep a check on how your assets are divided and keep a lid on the risk you have undertaken to bear.*

5 Rules to Remember

1. *Decide whether it's more important to eat well or to sleep well.*
2. *History shows that risk and return are related.*
3. *The longer you hold stocks and bonds, the lower the risk.*
4. *Find the middle ground between your investment style and recommended asset allocations for your age and lifestyle.*
5. *Rebalancing your portfolio can reduce risk.*

Chapter 16

Getting the Most out of Shares

Thanks to Internet broking, buying shares is becoming easier and easier. But these are still dangerous waters to navigate if you don't know what you're doing, so we'll spend a little time in this next section describing the pros and cons of different ways of buying shares. There are three main ways to do it:

1. Invest in an index-linked fund.
2. Choose your stocks yourself.
3. Hire a professional to manage your money for you.

Index funds

In a nutshell, an index fund is a mutual fund that invests in the companies that appear in a certain index. The Vanguard 500 Index Trust, for example, is linked to Standard & Poor's 500-Stock Index.

Because index funds follow the market so closely, you won't be far behind any trends and your investment portfolio reacts instantly to sudden changes. This makes index funds one of the simplest and safest ways to invest in stocks.

The advantages of index funds

An index fund operates in a similar way to pooled investment groups like actively managed funds, but with certain key differences. In an actively managed mutual fund, certain costs are always in place and management fees can take a hefty chunk out of your lump investment sum. In order to make it worth your while to invest in a fund like this, the stocks the fund invests in on your behalf will have to do very well.

> **EXAMPLE:**
>
> *If you invest a sum of $2,000 in an actively managed mutual fund, you might expect to pay 2.5% of that in management fees.*
>
> *2.5% of $2,000 is $50. The amount invested on your behalf is only $1,950.*
>
> *Your stocks will have to increase in value by 2.5% just to offset the management costs you have paid. They'll need to rise even higher to make a profit.*

Unlike actively managed mutual funds, index funds carry no trading costs or management fees, which makes them considerably less expensive than actively managed funds. Stocks don't have to increase in value as much to make you a profit, which means they're generally better performing—often by more than 1 or 1.5%.

The other key advantage is simplicity. Once you have chosen your index, the portfolio is automatically rebalanced to reflect the changes in stock value as per the index. Badly performing stocks that fail to keep their place in the top 500 (if your index is Standard & Poor's 500) will be replaced in your portfolio by stocks that do make the grade.

Choosing your funds

Don't invest in just a single index fund. It makes more sense to buy shares in a selection of funds that are designed to track the sorts of stock that form your investment portfolio.

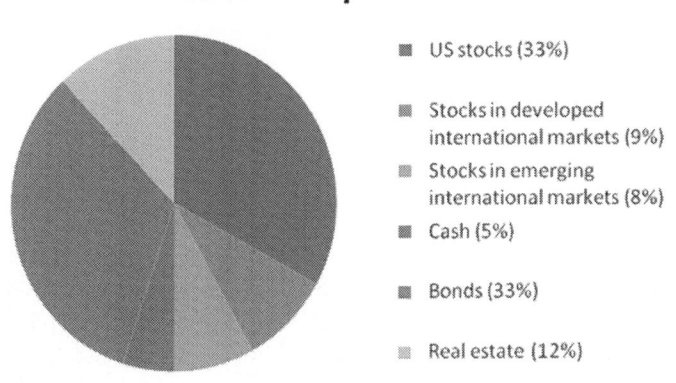

Imagine your portfolio looks like this:

Investment portfolio

- US stocks (33%)
- Stocks in developed international markets (9%)
- Stocks in emerging international markets (8%)
- Cash (5%)
- Bonds (33%)
- Real estate (12%)

Stocks of different classes make up 50% of your investment portfolio. You would need to match the different class of stocks to an index fund that tracks that particular class. The following is an example of different index funds and the types of stocks they track, plus how you might split your investment among them:

Stock class	Percentage of investment	Index funds
US stocks	33%	- T. Rowe Price - Vanguard Total Stock Market Fund Index
Stocks in developed international markets	9%	- Fidelity Spartan - Vanguard International Index Fund
Stocks in emerging international markets	8%	- Vanguard Emerging Markets Index Fund

Recommendation

Small index funds such as Standard & Poor's 500 track only the most established companies. Use a broader index such as Russell 3,000 or the Dow / Wilshire 5,000-Stock Index which include the smaller dynamic companies too.

Reduce risk by diversifying

High-quality US common stocks behave differently from stocks in emerging markets. Both will flourish under different conditions, which means that the risks associated with one can sometimes offset those that come with the other. Spread your investment across "safe" investments in US stocks and those from developed international markets, but make sure emerging market stocks have a place in your portfolio too.

Indexes to go by

Stock class	Index
US common stocks	- Dow / Wilshire 5,000 - Russell 3,000 - MSCI broad US index
Emerging markets	- Morgan Stanley Capital International (MSCI) - Index of European Australasian, Far Eastern (EAFE) securities - MSCI emerging markets index.

Index funds at a glance

Advantages:

- *Regularly produce higher rates of return than actively managed funds*
- *Tax friendly—realization of capital gains can be deferred*
- *Simple to manage*
- *Relatively low risk*
- *A good option for the small investor that still achieves broad diversification*

Disadvantages:

- *The popularity of index funds can make stocks pricier—opt for broader indexes to keep costs low*

Chapter 17

Choosing Your Own Shares

If you're something of a daredevil, you may prefer to choose your own portfolio of stocks rather than linking them to an index fund. It's perfectly possible to accumulate wealth in this way, and many people do successfully choose their own stocks. This strategy isn't recommended for beginners, however, and there are a few golden rules to remember to protect yourself:

1. Remember the difference between speculating and investing.

Choosing your own stocks to invest in works best if you adopt a buy and hold strategy. Trying to beat the market thanks to clever timing has ended in misery for legions of unsuccessful former day traders. Remember the unfortunate souls who sank their investment into the South Sea Company.

2. Only invest in companies or ventures that demonstrate sustainable capacity for growth over a period of five years or more.

Five years is a rough benchmark for confidence in a company's prospects. It demonstrates growth potential underpinned by some level of security, which will be attractive to other investors and push share prices up.

3. If the market price exceeds the true value, don't buy.

As we have seen, market values can fluctuate dramatically and don't necessarily represent a company's intrinsic value. If you believe a company is worth a certain sum, chances are that over time the market will average out at this foundation value.

4. Buy stocks with a good story as well as firm foundation value.

Good stories are what help whip up public expectation. If you sense that a particular company's stock has an inspiring story behind it, take the opportunity to contribute to the anticipation.

5. Only choose your own stocks if you can absorb the risk.

This method of investing is tricky and takes a good deal of luck as well as expertise. You'll need plenty of time to investigate your potential investments and this kind of research will need to be ongoing if you're to choose wisely. If you can absorb the risk of potential failure, then you may find a venture like this rewarding. If you can't, steer clear!

Where to find out more

Newspapers and journals

Financial publications are usually the most up-to-date and trustworthy sources of the latest market figures. They also usually include insightful features into certain companies and industries, so they are well worth looking at regularly. You might want to consider:

- The New York Times
- The Wall Street Journal
- Barron's
- Businessweek
- Fortune
- Forbes

Advisory services

Advisory services such as Standard & Poor's Outlook and the Value Line Investment Survey are excellent sources of information and advice about your next investment.

Chapter 18

Professional Management

In certain circumstances, such as when you have a question about your tax bill or when you are getting a mortgage, professional advice is necessary and sometimes even a legal requirement. When used properly, it can save you money in the long run and offer protection if you run into difficulties.

When choosing a portfolio of stocks, some people prefer to invest in an actively managed mutual fund. This means that rather than following an index, a human being decides on the number and type of shares that are bought and sold.

> **Professional management at a glance**
>
> *Advantages:*
> - Reduced paperwork
> - Increased diversification
> - Automatic reinvestment of profits
>
> - *Disadvantages:*
> - Management fees, commission, and expenses fees are payable whether you make a profit or not.
> - Past performance is no indicator or future success.

Now, that human being may be exceptionally gifted, insightful, and able to make the best possible decision on your behalf. Then again, every human has their faults, whether that's the lure of commission or simple laziness. Human managers also need to be paid for their time—and rightly so. The trick is to weigh up the advantages against the disadvantages.

The advantages of active management

The main advantage of an actively managed fund is that you get to do away with all the time-consuming paperwork. Your profits, losses, profile rebalancing, and asset allocation decisions are all made for you by a professional who is familiar with how the market works. This saves you time and frees you up to do what you want to do.

Many funds offer attractive extras such as automatic reinvestment of any dividends you earn. This means your profits are continually reinvested and you can watch your money grow more quickly thanks to compounding.

Managed funds also offer high levels of diversification, which not only spreads the risk you assume but helps your money go farther by investing it in multiple income streams rather than relying on the profits from just a few assets.

The disadvantages of active management

The main disadvantage of managed funds is that you will have to pay management fees whether you make any money from the service or not. And there really is no guarantee that you will make a profit. A good track record may be some indication of a fund's reliability and trustworthiness, but it's still no indicator of future performance.

Beware of the self-congratulatory advertisement slogans adopted by many funds. A surprising proportion of them claim to be "Number 1 for performance." They can't all be Number 1, or the position would be meaningless. Dig a little deeper and you may discover that this particular fund was "Number 1" for a three-month period in a specific asset class, but the rest of the time it performs just slightly above average compared to similar funds.

Put like that, it's not so impressive, is it?

The costs explained

Managed funds come with two main fee classifications: fees and expense charges.

Fees
Front-end load is a commission charge paid upfront—when you first purchase your stocks. The front-end load charge can be as high as 5%

and is quite unnecessary, so if you come across a fund that levies this charge, avoid it.

Back-end load is a charge incurred when you redeem your stocks. Typically, it's about 1%, depending on when you sell your shares. The later you sell it, the smaller the charge will be.

Exchange fees are incurred if you swap your shares for others within the same mutual fund. These fees are almost always a flat rate.

Expense charges

Expense charges are designed to cover the total operating costs of the fund—including advisory fees. The **expense ratio** expresses these fees as a percentage of the fund's average net assets. For index funds, this figure is roughly 1/10% per year. For actively managed funds, it can be as high as 2%—20 times higher than the costs incurred from an index fund.

> ## *Insight*
>
> *High fees lead to poorer investment performance because the higher the fees, the better the shares have to perform to make good your original investment. To protect your investment, opt only for funds with low fees.*

Recap:
The Three Methods of Buying Stocks

Index funds

- *An index fund is a mutual fund that invests in the companies that appear in a certain index, such as Standard & Poor's 500-Stock Index.*
- *Index funds regularly produce higher rates of return than actively managed funds.*
- *They are a good option for the small investor and still achieve broad diversification.*
- *The popularity of index funds can make stocks pricier—opt for broader indexes to keep costs low.*

Choosing your own stocks

Remember the golden rules:

- *Remember the difference between speculating and investing.*
- *Invest only in companies or ventures that demonstrate sustainable capacity for growth over a period of five years or more.*
- *If the market price exceeds the true value, don't buy.*
- *Buy stocks with a good story as well as firm foundation value.*
- *Choose your own stocks only if you can absorb the risk.*

Professional management

- *Actively managed funds reduce paperwork and record keeping.*
- *Some mutual funds offer special services such as automatic reinvestment.*
- *Load fees and expense charges mean that your stock has to perform very well before you can break even.*
- *A good track record is no indicator of future performance.*

Chapter 19

Real Estate

A successful man is one who can lay a firm foundation with the bricks that others throw at him.
– Sidney Greenberg

Real Estate is a good investment partly because it offers the security and independence of owning your own home, and partly because Real Estate assets tend to perform in a different way from other investments, making them a good diversifier and a hedge against risk.

You can make money from Real Estate whatever the market trend—whether it's up, down, or even sideways! But in order to do that, you need to understand what factors influence the market and how you can turn each trend to your advantage.

Understanding the Market

Interest rates

When interest rates are high, so is the cost of a mortgage. This means that fewer people will be able to afford a large mortgage and will prefer to rent. The lack of demand will generally lower house prices. By contrast, when interest rates are low, so are mortgage rates, and demand rises. Knowing the direction of interest rates can help you anticipate which way the housing market is headed.

Inflation

The cost of living—including renting—is linked to inflation. Longer-term investments such as Real Estate are considered a safe haven from fluctuations in inflation, except in extreme circumstances.

Macro-economy

An expanding national economy usually translates into more money for investment in Real Estate on an individual level too.

External influencing factors

It isn't purely market trends that have an impact on Real Estate prices. Other elements include:

Job growth and migration

More people coming into an area means an increased demand for houses, which will drive house prices up.

Development plans

New shopping centers, schools, and office buildings can generate interest in an area and attract more people to it, which will increase house prices.

Neighborhood trends

Some neighborhoods become trendy and vibrant quickly, particularly in large cities. Once new bars and meeting places open up, prices will follow the trend.

Making the most of the current trend

Careful examination of the factors previously listed will give you an understanding of whether the market is up or down. There will be opportunities to be seized, whichever way it's headed, as long as you employ the right strategy.

When the market is up – find properties to fix and sell quickly. You will add value to the property and profit from the upward market trend. If you think the market has reached a peak and will probably start to go down, look for highly motivated sellers and make an offer which is lower than their asking price. Once you've bought the property, rent it and wait for the market to go up again.

When the market is down – look for great deals from sellers who are keen to get rid of their properties. A few examples are new unsold homes, distressed properties, bank-owned properties, and tax sales. Pick the best bargains and rent them until the market recovers.

5 Rules to Remember

1. When interest rates are high, so is the cost of a mortgage. Lack of demand lowers house prices.

2. Real Estate is an asset protected from the effects of fluctuating interest rates.

3. Job growth, migration, and neighborhood trends affect house prices.

4. When the market is up, find properties to fix up and sell quickly.

5. When the market is down, look for deals from owners who are anxious to sell quickly.

Chapter 20

Achieving Your Goals through Smart Investing

Keep away from people who try to belittle your ambitions. Small people always do that, but the really great make you feel that you, too, can become great.
– Mark Twain

In Part 1, we asked you to take a moment to decide what you really want from life and to set some goals to help you achieve that. We're going to revisit some of those goals now and examine how you can achieve them with straightforward, easy steps.

Goal number 1: Saving for college

College fees are one of the highest individual costs any parents will be expected to meet. The fees can reach eye-watering levels—as much as $58,334 a year for the priciest (in this case, Sarah Lawrence College in Yonkers, NY).

But don't let the cost of tuition put you off. There are various avenues you can explore in the way of scholarships and need-based financial grants intended to help students from poorer backgrounds get the education they deserve.

In the meantime, let's look at some of the investment options available to you. Saving for college is a long-term investment and requires a growth strategy as opposed to protecting income that exists already. An ideal investment plan for this sort of long-term project allows you to put money into an investment vehicle that repays you your original investment plus the profits you've earned along the way on a specific date in the future. That way, you aren't tempted to spend the money, and it's kept separate from your other investments.

The two best methods of achieving this are bonds and a 529 savings account.

Zero coupon bonds

Zero coupon bonds are excellent vehicles for putting money aside that will be required at a specific future date. Ordinarily when you invest in bonds, you receive periodic interest payments which you can either put in a savings account or reinvest in bonds or stocks as you please. With zero coupon bonds, these interest payments are held back until the bond matures, meaning that you end up with a lump sum comprised of your original investment plus the profits it has earned up to maturity.

> *EXAMPLE:*
>
> *You buy a bond with a face value of $10,000.*
>
> *The bond's annual rate of return is 6%, or $600.*
>
> *You hold the bond for 12 years. At the end of this period, you receive the original sum of $10,000, plus $7,200 (12 X $600). Your total sum is $17,200.*

Discounted bonds

If you can, buy securities like these at a discount and let them gradually rise to their face value. With high-quality bonds such as Treasury Bills, there is no reinvestment risk and they come with a guarantee that funds will be reinvested at the yield to maturity rate.

529 savings account

A 529 savings account is designed specifically for saving for college tuition fees and allows parents and grandparents to make cash gifts to children for the purposes of college education.

An account like this comes with important tax breaks: Individual contributors are allowed to deposit up to $60,000 without incurring gift taxes. For couples, the limit is $120,000.

Funds in this savings account can be invested in stocks and bonds and there are no federal taxes on the earnings from this investment as long as the withdrawals are used only for higher education purposes.

There are a couple of warning bells that need to be sounded here. The first regards high commissions charged by sales people for these funds. Low-expense alternatives (from Vanguard and TIAA-CREER, for example) do exist, so it's worth shopping around before committing yourself.

The second thing to be aware of is that colleges take into account the earnings and deposits from a 529 plan when they consider applicants for need-based financial aid. By keeping 529 plans in your own name rather than your child's, you may be able to avoid this pitfall and still qualify for financial assistance as long as your earnings are under a certain threshold.

Recap: Saving for college – investment plans	
Asset type	Summary
Zero coupon bonds	<ul><li>Period dividend payments are suspended in favor of a lump sum paid on a specific date.</li><li>Safe, long-term investment</li><li>Treasury bonds guarantee reinvestment at the yield-to-maturity rate.</li></ul>
529 savings account	**Advantages:** <ul><li>No federal taxes</li><li>$60,000 individual contribution limit and $120,000 for couples</li><li>Can be invested in stocks and bonds</li></ul>**Disadvantages:**<ul><li>Beware high commissions from sales people</li><li>Can be taken into account during assessment for need-based financial assistance</li></ul>

Goal number 2: Buying a home

Buying a home is the single largest investment that most people make during their lives. A home is really quite an extraordinary asset: Property generally increases in value over time (as long as you look after it), and you can fix it up, rent it out, or live in it while it appreciates.

Saving toward a deposit and your mortgage payments provides many people with a concrete reason to start saving. Owning your own home is an emotional impulse as well as a rational one, so it provides a real reason to kick-start your investment strategy.

Saving is the cornerstone in your action plan for buying a home. The first and most important thing you can do is set up a regular savings plan.

There is an element of timeliness about buying: Generally you need to make an offer reasonably quickly and be prepared to follow through on the sale if it is accepted. This means you need to balance keeping your money accessible with longer-term strategies that offer higher rewards.

Let's say you set yourself the goal of saving $20,000 in five years.

Assuming an average yearly return of 5%, you need to save around $3,250 per year ($270 per month) in order to meet your target. Split your monthly investment between liquid assets such as high-interest saver accounts and CDs, and medium-term investments such as money-market mutual funds.

Money-market mutual funds

These funds are designed for medium-term investments of around three years and offer higher returns than your average bank account. The stick in the mud is that most require a minimum initial investment of between $2,000 and $3,000. If you don't have that kind of money up front, never fear—some mutual fund companies such as TIAA-CREF and Vanguard offer funds with low minimums—between $500 and $1,000.

Once you choose a mutual fund, you need to decide what your monthly investment should be. Returns depend on the performance of the fund, but on average you can expect a return of between 3% and 5%. The following depicts what would happen to an initial investment of $500 and monthly investments of $100 over a three-year period. For the sake of this exercise, we'll assume a return of 4%.

Year	Year deposits	Total deposits	Yearly interest	Cumulative interest	Total amount
1	$1,200	$1,200	$68	$68	$1,768
2	$1,200	$2,400	$118.72	$186.72	$3,086.72
3	$1,200	$3,600	$171.47	$358.19	$4,458.19

Example savings portfolio

Percentage allocation across assets

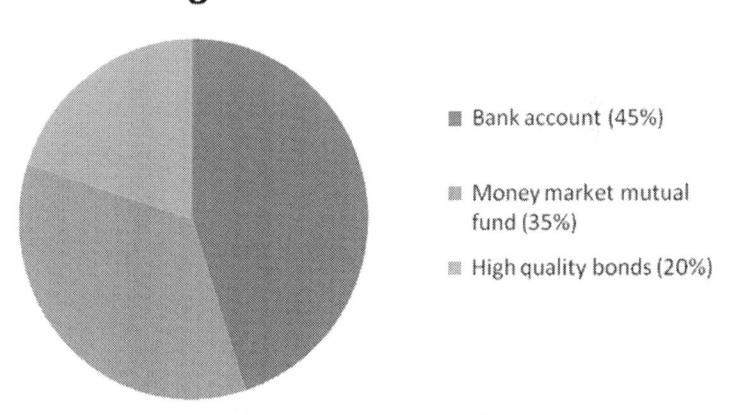

- Bank account (45%)
- Money market mutual fund (35%)
- High quality bonds (20%)

Goal number 3: Planning for retirement

Planning for your retirement is one of the most significant investments you will make in your life. The earlier you start, the easier it is to make sure that you have a comfortable stock of savings to fall back on when you stop working.

There are certain specific investment vehicles designed with retirement savings specifically in mind. These offer particular advantages such as tax breaks which allow you to make the most of the earnings you accumulate without having to wave goodbye to a large chunk of them. Let's have a look at some of these plans.

Individual Retirement Accounts (IRAs)

IRAs allow a yearly investment of around $5,000 which can be paid into your account without being taxable. If you have moderate earnings—in other words, you're in the 28% tax bracket—IRAs can be an excellent vehicle for your savings. You don't pay any tax on earnings gained from funds deposited in an IRA; instead, you just pay tax when you withdraw your funds. This is called "**tax-deferred investing**."

Roth IRAs

Roth IRAs come in two types: "**jam today**" and "**jam tomorrow.**" Jam today means that you get an immediate tax deduction on your initial investment but pay taxes when you withdraw funds. Jam tomorrow means that you get no initial tax deduction, but aren't liable for tax when you withdraw your funds.

Roth IRAs are best for people who are either far from retirement and in a low tax bracket, or closer to retirement but whose earnings are too high to allow them to qualify for a regular IRA.

Pension plans

If you're in employment

Plans **401(k)** and **403(b)** are available to anyone in employment. These plans are taxed at source, which means that your contributions to your pension plan are taken out of your gross salary, and you may deposit $15,000 per year before you are liable to pay any tax.

If you're self-employed

People who are self-employed are entitled to a **Keogh pension plan**, which allows you to invest up to 25% of your earnings per year, tax free. You're also entitled to a Keogh plan if you have a regular job but earn side income from a different source to your main job. Much like an IRA, any earnings you make on the funds you deposit into this plan are not taxable until they're withdrawn.

Recap: Saving for retirement – investment plans	
Asset type	Summary
IRAs	<ul><li>Save up to $5,000 per year</li><li>No upfront tax on earnings</li><li>Only pay tax when money withdrawn</li></ul>**Roth IRAs**<ul><li>Jam today offers immediate tax deduction, but you are taxed when you withdraw your funds.</li><li>Jam tomorrow offers no tax deduction, but you pay no tax when you withdraw your funds.</li></ul>
Pension plans	**401(k) & 403(b)**<ul><li>These plans are provided by employers.</li><li>Taxed at source</li><li>$15,000 per year contribution tax free</li></ul>**Keogh plan (for self-employed people)**<ul><li>25% of your annual earnings can be invested tax free.</li><li>Earnings are only taxed when withdrawn.</li></ul>

A final word

Over the course of the last chapter, you learned to identify your capacity for risk and came to grips with different ways of allocating your investment portfolio. You now know that specific investment vehicles usually perform best for specific goals in terms of offering important tax breaks, for example.

By following the simple rules we've just outlined, you will be in the best possible position to make informed decisions about how to make your money work for you.

In the final part of this book, we investigate how to do something that has given investors across the world the freedom to make a life, not just a living—start your own business.

PART 6

STARTING YOUR OWN BUSINESS

You make a living by what you earn; you make a life by what you give.

– Winston Churchill

Now that you are familiar with the basics of investment, you can start to put this knowledge to work in any way you like. One wonderful example is to start your own business. It gives you the freedom to make your own decisions and see your ideas come to life. It's an opportunity not only to express the things that make you tick, but to shape the world around you.

For those who manage to do it successfully, starting your own business can generate a comfortable income too. Some people make more than just a comfortable living—they make a fortune.

You don't even have to stick to a single business idea—you can run with several! Many people sell off the whole or part of a business in order to move into new sectors and try new things. Richard Branson is just one example.

Richard Branson's story

At the age of 20, Richard Branson founded a mail order record service called Virgin. A short while later, he opened a record shop on Oxford Street, London. After two years, inspired by the success of his record business, Branson formed the Virgin Records music label, which released its first record "Tubular Bells" in 1973.

This album sold more than five million copies.

Richard Branson went on to sign The Sex Pistols to Virgin Records after the group was rejected by every other record label in Britain. Since then, Virgin Records has signed superstars including Genesis, Phil Collins, Janet Jackson, and The Rolling Stones.

From an internationally acclaimed music label, Virgin has expanded into air and rail travel, finance, cell phones, and retail—with over 200 companies to its name.

Richard Branson is just one example of a successful entrepreneur. His success is due to his ability to spot potential niches in the market for a new idea or a new project—and not to be put off by the risk of plunging into the unknown.

You can learn these skills too, and we cover some of them in this chapter. You will learn:

- ✓ How to minimize your workload using the 80/20 principle
- ✓ What makes a successful business
- ✓ How to become a leader
- ✓ How to identify market niches
- ✓ How to make a sale
- ✓ How to market yourself
- ✓ How to establish systems that will decrease your workload

Your business is the most vibrant and exciting of your multiple income streams. It does carry some risk, but you can manage this risk in exactly the same way that you would weigh up the benefits of simple saving against longer-term investments.

A business is a long-term investment, so it will need proper planning, care, and attention in order to grow and flourish. In this chapter, we show you how.

Chapter 21

The 80/20 Principle

Never leave that till tomorrow which you can do today.
– Benjamin Franklin

In 1897, the Italian economist Vilfredo Pareto identified an imbalance between the inputs and the results of any system. This phenomenon became known as the 80/20 principle—where 80% of the results are generated by 20% of the input. The following are some examples:

- 80% of the world's GDP is generated by 20% of the population.
- 80% of profit comes from 20% of customers.
- 80% of complaints come from 20% of customers.
- 80% of crimes are committed by 20% of criminals.
- 80% of sales come from 20% of products.

If you can focus on the 20% of the factors that generated 80% of the results, you can benefit from a number of long-term advantages:

- Increased productivity
- The ability to concentrate on what matters most
- The ability to accomplish more but work less

Using the 80/20 principle in your business

Starting your own business is a great opportunity to put the 80/20 principle into practice. In practical terms, it means focusing on the things that you can do most effectively and outsourcing the rest.

Some examples of the 80% of tasks that generate minimal success:

- Tasks you are not skilled at
- Tasks you don't enjoy
- Interrupted and incomplete tasks
- Answering the phone

- Things few other people share an interest in

Some examples of the 20% of tasks that are worth doing

- Things you have always wanted to do
- Getting people to do the things you don't want to do
- Tasks that are directly related to your purpose in life
- Urgent tasks
- Tasks related to your creativity
- Working with people you admire and who are highly productive

Getting into good habits

In Part 1, we talked about adopting a positive mindset and setting achievable goals for yourself. I want you to remember this now because the 80/20 principle can not only achieve greater productivity (and greater prosperity) for your business, it can make you happier too.

Time management

According to Pareto and to Parkinson's Law, a task will swell in importance and complexity in relation to the time allotted for its completion. Most people have experienced this phenomenon in some way—particularly when tackling a task they find difficult. It's human nature to put off doing difficult tasks, but putting them off comes with the inevitable consequence that they tend to take far more time than is necessary and limit the opportunity for working on more profitable and enjoyable challenges.

Being efficient doesn't mean that you squeeze as much work as possible into your day. It means that you identify the time-wasters and get rid of them.

Multitasking is a particular bad egg: Many people believe that by doing several things at once they are savings themselves time. Actually, they are less efficient because they fail to give each task its due attention. The result is shoddy results and incomplete tasks that need tackling later.

6 Rules for success

1. *Identify the things that make you happiest and spend more time on them.*
2. *Identify the things that make you the least happy and structure your life to avoid them as much as possible.*
3. *Maximize the proportion of your life under your direct control.*
4. *Set goals that are achievable for a sense of accomplishment.*
5. *Cultivate a few close, positive, and happy friends.*
6. *Focus on emphasizing your strengths and improving your weaknesses.*

Selective ignorance saves you time

In today's world of smartphones and instant access to information, many of us spend hours on unproductive tasks such as checking and replying to e-mails as they come in. Identifying time-sapping activities like these will help you cut back on unnecessary jobs. Timothy Ferriss' book *The 4-Hour Workweek* advises readers to ignore everything that is unimportant. Avoid trivial and worthless information and get rid of anything that wastes your time. The following are some rules to remember:

1. Check e-mails just twice a day and delete as much as possible.
2. Have two phone numbers: one which goes directly to voicemail (so that you can deal with calls in a batch) and one which you give to only a small group of people for emergencies.
3. Schedule face-to-face meetings in advance and leave the room at the time they are scheduled to finish.
4. Batch similar activities together to minimize time losses.

By following these simple rules, you will be more productive, less stressed, and better able to concentrate your energies on the task at hand.

Recap: The 80/20 Principle

1. *20% of factors generate 80% of results.*

2. *The 80/20 principle can save you time and make both your business and your personal life happier and more successful.*

3. *The 80% of unproductive tasks include tasks you are not skilled at, don't enjoy doing, and interrupted tasks.*

4. *The 20% of productive tasks include things you enjoy, tasks that are directly related to your purpose in life, urgent issues, and working with people you admire.*

5. *Putting off difficult tasks means only that they will grow in time and importance.*

6. *Selective ignorance can save you time.*

Chapter 22

Bricks and Mortar – How a Business Is Constructed

Vision without action is daydream.
Action without vision is nightmare.
– Japanese proverb.

Your business is a multifaceted thing. Teams of people with distinct and complementary skills come together to achieve one thing—your company mission. Let's take a look at the different building blocks of a company.

Your mission

A company's mission is its raison d'être—its entire reason for being. It touches the spirit and spurs you and your employees on through the difficult times. It provides fire, passion, and drive, and helps you keep focused during the good times.

The best missions provide an emotional stimulus that involves the customer. Take Henry Ford's, for example:

"Democratize the automobile"

Henry Ford identified a gap in the market for affordable cars that could be more widely available to the general public, not just the super-rich. He set up a company to fulfill that need.

Why is this mission statement so powerful?

It may sound obvious, but part of the reason this mission (or vision) is successful is that it's short. Short statements are memorable and more likely to create a lasting impact than complex ones. Next, it demonstrates the desire for change for the better, and the power to bring it about. Finally, the statement is inclusive. Democratizing the automobile makes it available as a product to everyone—and by that I really mean everyone. By not pigeonholing his audience, Henry Ford opened the way to appealing to all types of potential customers.

Your team

A business is a team sport, and it simply isn't possible to do everything by yourself. Look at it this way: If you run a bakery, you need a baker, a shop assistant to sell the cakes, and someone to oversee the finances. Would you employ the same person to do all three jobs? Of course not. Your financial wizard may know nothing about baking, but he will keep your accounts in perfect order. Your shop assistant may know nothing about finances, but he understands how to treat his customers. Each brings a unique skill to his job.

In the same way, you may know enough about each set of skills to be able to manage a team of people, but you aren't necessarily the best person to actually do the baking, even if you have a rough knowledge of it.

In a team of people, knowledge is shared and it grows. The beauty of this is that you get a sort of intellectual security which increases with the size of the company as more people bring their knowledge and skills to the table.

Systems management

In the same way that members of your team work together to bring about your company mission, systems help support the day-to-day business you undertake. Each system may have a specific purpose but it links with others to achieve a common goal. Systems ensure a solid working approach across the board to make sure your company runs as efficiently as possible. Typical systems include operations, product development, billing and accounting, customer service, marketing, HR, and resource management.

Leadership

Leadership is a skill you will need to learn to be successful in business. Good leaders are able to inspire their teams and achieve more than those who are overly forceful or too weak. The best business leaders have a mix of formal education and street smarts, stay focused on the mission, welcome feedback, and listen to their teams. They seek to bring out the best in people. Sometimes being a leader means making tough decisions—you have to be prepared to take the rap for whatever choices you make.

Communication

Good communication is vital. Communicating well with your team means that your vision can be shared and problems minimized. Communication with potential customers is a key ingredient to ensuring your business can continue by providing people with the products and services they need.

Cash flow

Cash flow is the life blood of your business. It allows you to develop a product, undertake research, cover overhead costs, and invest in future projects. You should review your financial situation regularly to anticipate future expenses and allocate your budget appropriately to ensure they are covered.

Chapter 23

Building a Successful Business

Be not afraid of greatness. Some are born great, some achieve greatness, and some have greatness thrust upon 'em.
– William Shakespeare

Starting your own business can have some great benefits: You can be your own boss, set your own goals, and make your own decisions. But how do you get started? What should your product be? What service should you offer?

Honestly, you can shape your business around whatever idea you like. Perhaps you want to start a bakery or open a bookshop. You could operate a photography company or provide musicians for corporate functions. Every one of these ideas has been done successfully in the past.

Whatever your idea, it must obey one golden rule: It must add value to people's lives. It must give them something they want or need, but don't have yet.

It's no good simply formulating a business around something that interests you if it doesn't offer something to your potential customers. The plain fact of the matter is that your business must sell its products. This means that you must offer products that fulfill a need in some way.

The five components of a successful business

Every successful business keeps five things in mind:

1. Value creation
2. Marketing and branding
3. Sales

4. Value delivery
5. Financial security

Value creation

We have already discussed value creation. This involves reaching the market to identify niches that you could fill.

Marketing

No matter how good your product is, it won't sell itself. You need to tell the world about it and demonstrate why your customers would benefit from buying. Part of marketing is creating a visual identity for your company, or in other words, establishing your brand. Your brand is the public face of your company, so it needs to convey your mission, build trust in your company, and inspire your customers.

The golden rule

> *Whatever your business idea, it must fulfill a need. It must offer a solution to a problem or add value to your customers' lives.*

Sales

Sales are the cornerstone of your business. They generate your income and are the difference between make or break for your company's future prospects.

Value delivery

Value delivery is all about delivering a product that does what you say it should. It's about quality control and creating (and keeping) customer satisfaction. Value delivery is vital for sustaining your brand's reputation and retaining your customers.

Financial security

The financial side of things means managing the nuts and bolts of your company, from catering for overhead costs and day-to-day expenses such as staff salaries and production costs, to deciding which pricing model is most appropriate for which product.

Value creation – Finding your niche

If you're starting a business, you have two options. The first is to do something completely original—something that no one else is doing. The second is to do something other people are doing—but do it better. Ultimately, your business' main reason for being isn't to make money, but to serve your customers. Concentrate on providing something that people need, and you'll have no trouble selling your product and making an income.

It comes down to finding niches—whether those are low-cost areas or unserved needs—and to do that, you need to evaluate the market.

How to evaluate a market

If you have a business idea in mind, you need to take a look at the environment you will be joining to establish whether or not there is space in the marketplace for it to flourish. You need to be aware of your competition (in the form of similar products and providers), the uniqueness of what you have to offer, how much similar products sell for, and how the logistics of creating, selling, and automating production can work.

Let's break it down a little.

Timing

The best-selling ideas are ones that meet an urgent need. Take a look around you. Do people really need your business? If they do, making your first sales will be that much easier.

Market size

The market size simply means the number of people who are buying a product similar to yours. If there is a clear demand for such a product, you can establish a potential buyer base without too much trouble. The skill will be to ensure that customers buy your particular product.

Uniqueness of offer

Assuming there is a market for your product, how unique is it? What is it about your particular product that will help it stand out from the crowd? Identifying your product's Unique Selling Proposition (USP) will help when it comes to marketing.

Costs

There are various unavoidable costs which you need to take into account and weigh up against the income you expect to make. These costs fall into three broad categories:

1. Upfront expenses (overheads, design, staff salaries)
2. Customer acquisition (marketing campaigns and advertising)
3. Value delivery (manufacturing and distribution)

Income

Determining the income you expect your product to make relies on having a fair understanding of what people are willing to pay for it. Investigate the going rate for similar products that already exist and weight your pricing accordingly.

Weighing up the risks

Now that you've had a look at the market around you and established a niche for your business, it's time to look at the nitty gritty. This means being very honest with yourself about the challenges and difficulties your business may face, and how you might overcome them.

There are two basic techniques that will help get you started. They are called **SWOT Analysis** and **Cost / Benefit Analysis.**

SWOT analysis

A SWOT analysis is one of the simplest and most effective ways of determining the potential success of your ideas and the opportunities you have to develop them.

Let's imagine for a moment that you want to open a coffee shop in a small town. The coffee shop's unique selling proposition is that it doubles up as an art shop and gallery selling work by local artists. Naturally, that coffee shop will be subject to different threats and opportunities depending on its location, the number of people who have access to it or know about its existence, and the presence of rival shops in the vicinity. Here's what a SWOT analysis might look for this shop:

STRENGTHS	WEAKNESSES
<ul><li>The shop's location (opposite the local park but close to the main high street)<ul><li>Easily accessible to shoppers</li><li>A pleasant place to relax with a view of the park</li></ul></li><li>There is no other coffee shop in the area which also sells art.</li><li>The town has a high proportion of retired people, many of whom have both money and time to spare.</li></ul>	<ul><li>Unpredictability (whether the coffee shop will be as popular as anticipated)</li><li>Potential high overheads (a larger space may be required to display paintings)</li><li>Significant startup capital is required to rent the premises.</li><li>Lack of commuter traffic in the mornings means that business relies on weekend shoppers.</li></ul>
OPPORTUNITIES	THREATS
<ul><li>Local artists have already expressed an interest in loaning their pieces to the shop.</li><li>Local news teams have agreed to cover the shop's opening in local papers and magazines.</li><li>A famous artist originally from your town has agreed to give a talk at the shop.</li></ul>	<ul><li>Rival shops may open close by and draw business away.</li><li>Sales may not outweigh startup costs.</li></ul>

This shop has the advantage of being one of a kind in a small town, which means competition will be pretty thin on the ground. The flipside is that there's no precedent for something of this kind, so it will be difficult to judge how it might fit into a small, established community.

Cost / Benefit analysis

A cost / benefit analysis breaks down some of the opportunities we discovered in the SWOT analysis by how much each component of the business will cost and whether or not the resulting benefits are enough to make up for these costs. It can help you:

- Decide whether a project is worthwhile
- Create a framework for your project objectives
- Set project goals and measures of success
- Estimate the resources you'll need to complete the project

Rules to remember

> *Everything should have a dollar value in a cost / benefit analysis. Sometimes it will be difficult to put a monetary value on the benefits you expect to see (such as the potential for a holiday to bring in more customers), but try to estimate the value to give you a fuller picture.*

Consider all the costs

A project may have both upfront costs (such as capital investment, labor, and installation costs) and recurring costs (maintenance and repair). It's important to consider all of these. You should also think about:

- The cost of not doing the project
- The cost if the project fails
- The cost of doing this project as opposed to a different one

> EXAMPLE:
>
> Let's imagine we are considering buying a frozen drinks dispenser for our coffee shop.
>
> **Upfront costs / income:**
>
> - Unit cost: $2,000
> - Cost of ingredients per cup: $2
> - Income from each cup sold: $4
> - Profits from each cup: $2
>
> We will need to sell 1,000 cups in order to earn back the price of the unit. Broken down over a year, a simple cost / benefit table looks like this:

Costs	Benefits
- $2,000 unit cost - $100 installation fee - $100 staff training costs - $2 for ingredients (each cup) @ 5,000 cup sales per year = $10,000 - $100 maintenance fee (per year) **Costs: $12,300**	- Each cup sells for $4 @ 5,000 cup sales per year = $20,000 - Additional customers drawn by frozen drinks = 500 per year ($2,000) - 10-year guarantee on equipment / free maintenance ($100 per year) **Income: $22,100**

TOTAL: +$9,800

In this case, buying the frozen drinks unit makes a potential profit, so it is worth pursuing.

If in doubt, do some research into the operating costs of businesses similar to yours. Which decisions worked best for them? Learn from their mistakes and successes.

Marketing

Marketing is a key ingredient to the success of any business. It's the name for the selection of tools that tell the world about your business, your product, and what your company stands for.

Building your brand

Your brand should reflect your reputation, aspirations, and company mission in a way that is instantly identifiable and easy to remember. It also needs to create a visual identity that separates you from your competitors. Branding includes:

- Your company mission statement or vision
- Your values (such as high quality at low prices)
- Your Unique Selling Proposition (USP)
- A visual identity (signature colors, logos, fonts, and imagery)

Good branding design helps draw the other elements together to create a coherent visual identity that helps potential customers identify you. It's also the first thing that most people see when they are introduced to your company. In the same way that you would dress neatly to create a good first impression at a job interview, good brand design is vital to establishing a visual identity your business can be proud of.

Elements of brand design

Logo

A logo is the corporate face of your business and needs to do four things:

1. Create immediate recognition for your brand
2. Convey your business' character (family-friendly / glamorous / cutting-edge)
3. Set your brand apart from your competitors
4. Inspire trust and loyalty

It can be tempting to try to achieve too much with a logo. Stick to simple messages; bold, short statements; and simple designs. It is better to make one clear statement than to say too much. Your choice of colors needs to work in the same way. The fewer colors the better: Two or three are okay—but no more—and choose tones that contrast clearly without clashing.

Signature colors

Your signature colors appear on your logo and any publicity materials associated with your business—from websites to e-mail marketing campaigns or print advertisements. Choose a primary palette of two contrasting colors for your headings and strong banner or background colors, and a secondary supporting palette of subtler colors to allow you the variety to branch out into more extensive design when you need it.

Most businesses have an online presence in the form of a website or social media page, so make sure the colors you use are accessible online. In other words, the contrast between the background and the font color needs to be strong enough to be easily read on screen. (Pale pink text on a white background is not a good idea.) Make a note of the HEX or RGB codes that correspond to your chosen colors to make sure you use exactly the same shade each time.

Signature fonts

Fonts can convey a lot of information about your company, so take care to choose an appropriate one. A financial services institution which presents its written documentation in **Comic Sans**, for example, is unlikely to be taken seriously. In a school or a company which manufactures children's clothes, however, this font is just fine.

Generally, the simpler and clearer the font, the better.

Warning:

> *Estimating future costs can be tricky, particularly if you have no previous pricing model to go on. The farther into the future you look, the more difficult it is to accurately predict the costs you will encounter and the income you can expect from your initial outlay.*

Deciding on your style

So how do you go about establishing a visual identity for your company? In an ideal world, you would hire a professional designer to work with you on this. But if you can't afford one, there are a few basic steps that will keep you from going too far wrong:

1. **Do your research.**

Make a list of statements you want people to associate with your company. For example: "This company is one I can trust." Take a look at the branding style used by companies who share your working ethos, or companies you admire. What makes their branding stand out?

2. **Create several alternative designs.**

You're unlikely to get it right the first time, so take the time to create three or four contrasting designs that reflect your company's aspirations and identity. It's a good idea to show these to as many people as you can—both inside and outside your business.

3. **Seek feedback.**

Once you've chosen a design, continue to ask for feedback about the impression it makes on your audience. It may take several months to get an accurate picture of how your design is performing, but once you start to understand what works and what doesn't, you'll be able to make little adjustments to improve your initial efforts.

Blowing your own trumpet

By now, you have a financially viable business idea and a visual identity which reflects your company's aims. Now it's time to let the world know you've arrived. Tempting though it may be to wait for the perfect product or until your company has completely established itself—don't! Everyone needs to start somewhere, and timing can be crucial when it comes to launching a new product or achieving success in the marketplace. Don't wait until the timing is perfect—it may never be.

If you have a product which is unlike anything already in the market, do your best to bring it to people's attention before anyone else does. People have a tendency to stick with the product they've got, so if you can, be first in the marketplace.

Marketing's golden rules

1. **Keep it simple.**

Customers want to know the selling points of your product with as little inconvenience to themselves as possible. Short, sharp, clear messages are infinitely preferable to long explanations.

2. **Be precise.**

Don't be generic or abstract. Highlight the benefits for your customers: If you're selling a phone, don't sell the phone itself, sell the ideals that the phone brings (conversations, connection, games, music).

3. **Do the opposite of your competitors.**

If you're a car manufacturer specializing in sedans, don't try to compete with other manufacturers in the same category. Say Mercedes Benz leads the way in elegant, four-door sedans. There's no point trying to compete with them by using the very same idea, so be the leader in sporty four-door sedans instead.

4. **Trial and error**

If a strategy is not working, don't try harder to make it work. Test different messages. Test different communication methods—from e-mail, to SMS marketing, to printed adverts in magazines. For most people, a combination of these approaches works well. You need to be prepared to change your approach to reflect what your audience is responding to.

5. **Remember your audience.**

Depending on your product, you might be marketing to a very specific audience, or a very broad one. If you're dealing with a broad target market, split it up into sections and treat each section differently. Use different messaging for different groups to ensure your communications are relevant.

Using different channels

Online

Online marketing covers everything from creating a website to e-mail campaigns and social media marketing using Facebook or Twitter. Your company's website is a vital hub of information for prospective clients or customers and an opportunity to really explain what your company is about. If you have a product to sell, you can offer an online shop which is cheaper to run than a physical store.

Four rules for creating a website:

1. Create a clear structure – your users should be able to find the information they are looking for with minimal effort.
2. Less is more – break lengthy text up into short paragraphs with clear headings.
3. Link between pages – create deep links in the body of your text to related pages elsewhere in the site to help visitors navigate their way around.
4. Use the whole page – choose a wide template so that you don't end up with redundant space.

Search engine optimization

Search engines index websites based on the information they find in text headings, image alt tags, and meta descriptions, as well as links to that website from external sources. Well-written, clear text is easiest for search engines to find. Make sure you use relevant keywords in your text headings.

E-mail campaigns

E-mail campaigns are an excellent marketing tool. Chances are you will have an audience of customers or potential customers that will react differently to different types of campaigns. For example, if you are trying to persuade people to sign up for an event, you may want to stress different benefits depending on whether your audience is male or female, old or young. Targeting your communications to people's specific interests makes your messaging more relevant.

Don't bombard people with e-mail communications, however—it's a real turn-off for your customers. You must also always give people the option to opt out of e-mail communications from your firm.

Social media marketing

Social media is growing fast: Twitter has around 200 million users and Facebook has well over 800 million. This is a huge base of people who might be interested in your business. These platforms are relatively cheap to use (setting up a Facebook page is free, for instance), and they are designed for targeted communication in real time. Networks like these are an ideal environment to spread news about a new product, research your competitors, and get feedback about how you're doing.

"Above the line"

"Above the line" marketing refers to communications designed to be seen by a large audience. This type of marketing incorporates channels such as print (e.g., magazines, newspapers, and billboards), radio, and television advertising.

Generally speaking, "above the line" communications are more expensive to implement than online campaigns, partly because of the volume of people they hope to reach, and partly because of the practical costs of producing physical materials for widespread distribution.

If you advertise on television, take care to schedule your slot within a program that might appeal to your audience. This means undertaking research to find out what makes your customer base tick.

Making a sale

In business, until you've made a sale, you ain't got nothing. A sale demonstrates the viability of your business idea, your investment decision, or your product. It provides you with the cash flow you need to continue investing or to expand your business. It's your raison d'être, your future, your ticket to success.

So how do you make a sale? A good starting point is to shift your focus from you—your business, your investments—to your potential customers.

Find out what people want.

Find out what your customers need and help them get it. You need to seek and accept feedback—even if it means taking rejection and hearing negative comments. Failure is a better teacher than success, so embrace your customers' opinions and learn from them.

Don't over-promise.

Never promise more than you can deliver. Customers have a right to have their expectations met, so it's up to you to set those expectations at a level you can achieve.

Focus on value.

Clearly communicate the reason your offer is valuable to the purchaser. Ultimately, you are selling a solution to a problem—your tool or service just happens to be that solution. Help your customers visualize the improvement in their lives once they've accepted your offer.

Know your industry, and praise your competitors.

Understanding your industry helps you keep ahead of it. It's important to understand and value your competitors: Praising their contribution demonstrates that you are secure in your own offering and able to appreciate excellence in others.

Find common ground.

Seek out the area in which your customers' interests overlap with your own. It's like dividing a cake—the trick is to persuade everyone that they have the largest piece.

Don't argue—ask questions.

Few people, particularly customers, will thank you for telling them that they are wrong. Never argue with a customer. Ask them questions to understand their needs and use their answers to offer them a better service—one that will suit them.

Take advantage of word of mouth.

Word of mouth is an excellent tool for making sales. Ask happy customers to recommend you to family and friends. A personal recommendation is far more powerful than any advertising campaign.

Going on autopilot

A business is a collection of interlinking systems that each achieve a different purpose but are linked to an overarching common goal. Systems are processes made explicit and repeatable; this means they can work on autopilot to a certain extent, drastically reducing the workload for you and your staff.

Of course, no one starts a business with a set of fully functioning systems in place. But you can split your operations out into different sections or departments, each responsible for a certain thing. The following is an example of an organization structure for a large restaurant:

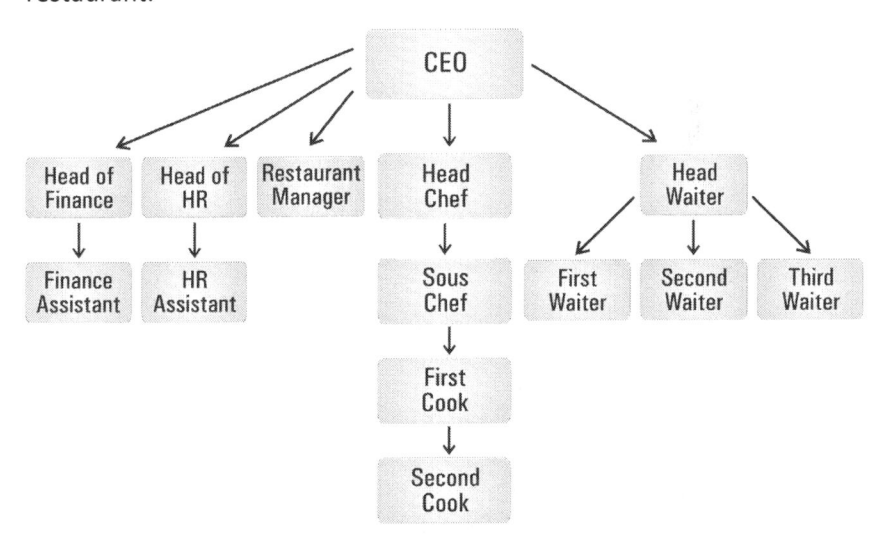

```
                            CEO
          ┌──────┬──────┬────┼────────────┐
          ↓      ↓      ↓    ↓            ↓
      Head of  Head of  Restaurant  Head     Head
      Finance   HR      Manager     Chef     Waiter
          ↓      ↓                   ↓      ┌──┼──┐
      Finance   HR                  Sous    ↓  ↓  ↓
      Assistant Assistant           Chef   First Second Third
                                     ↓     Waiter Waiter Waiter
                                   First
                                   Cook
                                     ↓
                                   Second
                                   Cook
```

Rather than trying to do everything, the CEO delegates responsibility to a team who are each expert in a particular field. They take over the day-to-day business of their particular department, leaving the CEO free to think more strategically about the business as a whole.

Within each department, more systems are created. Let's take the chefs, for example. In a restaurant that contains 30 diners at any one time, it would be impossible for the head chef to make every individual meal himself. Instead he might assign specific tasks to his team so that the sous chef is in charge of sauces, the first cook is in charge of meats, and the second is in charge of desserts. Each person follows his particular set of instructions without getting in the others' way and all the tasks that need to be done are done.

Financial security

Now that your business is up and running, it's vital to keep a close eye on your accounts. In order to make a profit, you need to keep a check on your business' running costs and save money where you can.

The following chart is a simple budget example for a small bakery. Your budget needs to include all fixed and variable costs over the course of the year. We included three months just to get you started:

	January	February	March
Income			
Sales	$7,000	$6,800	$7,200
TOTAL INOME	**$7,000**	**$6,800**	**$7,200**
Variable costs			
Raw materials	$400	$500	$450
TOTAL VARIABLE COSTS	**$400**	**$500**	**$450**
Fixed costs			
Staff salaries	$3,000	$3,000	$3,000
Rent	$1,500	$1,500	$1,500
Electricity, heat, water	$50	$50	$50
Stationary telephone	$20	$20	$20
Internet connection	$20	$20	$20
Website subscription/hosting & upgrading	$10	$10	$10
Marketing /advertising	$50	$50	$50
Equipment maintenance	$0	$0	$0

Unexpected costs (5% of costs)	$235	$235	$235
TOTAL FIXED COSTS	$4,923.50	$4,923.50	$4,923.50
TOTAL PROFIT	$2076.50	$1,876.50	$2,278.50

Defining pricing to make a profit

Part of keeping your business financially healthy is charging the right price for your products. Charge too little and you sell yourself short, but charge too much, and you may put potential customers off.

A simple pricing model takes into account:

- Replacement cost – the cost of build plus mark-up
- Market comparison – the price of similar items in the market
- Net present value – how much cash flow your product generates
- Value comparison – identifying groups for whom this product might carry particular value

Chapter 24

Becoming a Leader

People who are crazy enough to think they can change the world, are the ones who do.
– Apple Computers

Being a leader means more than simply calling the shots. It's about developing the skills to deal with people so that they can deliver their potential and work together for a positive outcome for the business.

Working with people, particularly if you're in charge, is rarely straightforward, but there are some good rules of thumb that will help guide you through these tricky waters.

Rules for good leadership

Avoid criticism and blame
It's easy to criticize, but this can have a negative impact on working relationships. People who feel themselves under criticism naturally become defensive, which can lead to resentment and impede a helpful resolution.

Put yourself in their shoes
Encouraging people to do what you want them to do is tricky. Rather than talking in terms of what you want, describe the benefit for them. When selling a product, for example, think of how your product can be a solution to their problems.

Call people by name
A person's name is important to them. Make an effort to learn people's names—they'll be more likely to respond to what you have to say.

Compromise
To achieve cooperation, invite people to put forward their own ideas. You can make suggestions, but ask them to draw their own conclusions.

If they feel responsibility and ownership for the decision, they will put more energy into it.

Empathize

People make mistakes. It's a fact of life. If you are able to empathize with the mistake and help the person who made it understand why it happened, they are less likely to make the same mistake a second time.

Give a reason for your actions

If you ask someone to do something, explain why you have done so. If they can see the benefit, they will feel as though you trust them enough to take the time to explain your thinking, and they will be more likely to support your decision.

Rules to remember for a successful business

Value creation

1. Businesses must fulfill a need. Remember that you are selling solutions, not products.

2. Evaluate the market and look at your competitors to find your niche—this could be an un-served need or a low-cost alternative to products already in existence.

3. Use a SWOT analysis to identify potential opportunities and threats.

4. Is it really worth it? Use a cost / benefit analysis to weigh up the risks of any project.

Marketing

1. Your brand is the public face of your company. It should reflect your vision and be instantly recognizable to your customers.

2. The visual elements of your brand include your logo, signature colors, signature fonts, and imagery.

3. Ask for feedback on your branding designs and be prepared to adapt.

4. Marketing is the collection of tools that brings your business to your customers' attention. Don't forget to:

    a) Keep your messaging clear and simple;

    b) Be precise about what you can offer;

    c) Offer something different from your competitors;

    d) Tailor your communications to your audience.

5. Use a variety of channels to communicate with your audience, including online, print, radio, and television.

Sales

1. Sales provide cash flow and generate the income you need for future development of your business.

2. Focus on your customers' needs rather than those of your business.

3. Manage expectations and don't over-promise.

4. Focus on the value you can offer customers.

5. Know your industry and your place in it.

Going on autopilot

1. A system is a process made explicit and repeatable.
2. A business is a collection of interlinking systems which have a common goal.
3. Delegation means that each person does what they are skilled at, reducing time wasting.

Financial security

1. Create a budget and stick to it.
2. When defining a product price, take into account:
    a) Replacement cost;
    b) Market comparison;
    c) Net value;
    d) Value comparison.

Leadership

1. Being a leader is not the same as being a boss.
2. Being a leader means helping your colleagues reach their potential.
3. Empathizing when mistakes happen can help to avoid them in future.

A final word

I hope you have found the information in this book useful. You now have the knowledge and skills to take control of your finances and achieve your goals. What you do with that knowledge is up to you. Perhaps you will start your own business, save to buy your own home, or invest in the stock market. It's your decision.

The advice you've encountered in this book is just a stepping stone in your financial journey. Keep learning, keep discovering, keep trying, and don't be afraid to make mistakes—they will help you find your path to success.

Remember that the only person in control of you is you. So don't put off doing what you want to do. Explore. Dream. Discover.

Congratulations—and good luck!

PART 7

WHERE TO FIND OUT MORE

Daily papers

The Wall Street Journal financial pages

Website: http://online.wsj.com/public/page/news-financial-markets-stock.html

The Wall Street Journal financial pages are a mine of information relating to market trends and the current performance of different commodities and mutual funds. The blogs offer accessible, insightful commentary.

The New York Times

Website: http://www.nytimes.com/

The Times offers news, business news, market data, and commentary.

The Financial Times

Website: http://www.ft.com/markets/

The markets section of the FT offers information on global funds, indexes, and market data.

Weekly papers/magazines

Barron's

Website: http://online.barrons.com/home-page

Barron's is one of the United States' most popular financial magazines and provides in-depth commentary on the markets. The online content is updated daily.

Businessweek

Website: http://www.businessweek.com/

Businessweek covers market trends and business news and offers insight into the lives of successful people.

Fortune

Website: http://money.cnn.com/magazines/fortune/

Fortune magazine is a subscription service offering commentary, market data, and business insights.

Forbes

Website: http://www.forbes.com/

Forbes covers news, financial information, politics, and economics, plus it offers opinion and insight pieces.

Advisory services

Standard & Poor's Outlook

Website: http://www.spoutlookonline.com/NASApp/NetAdvantage/SPO/home.jsp

The Outlook is a subscription service providing information for the individual investor.

Value Line Investment Survey

Website: http://www.valueline.com/

Research hub and reporting service designed to help investors get the most from their investment choices. It has an excellent set of training pages for those who are new to report making and investing.

The Morningstar Mutual-Fund Information Service

Website: http://www.morningstar.com/

In the early 1990s, Dan Phillips initiated the Morningstar service, which publishes information on mutual funds. Here you'll find everything from risk ratings and past returns, to sales charges, expense rations, and portfolio composition.

Mutual funds

Mutual Fund overview

Website: https://www.fidelity.com/mutual-funds/overview

This site provides commentary and comparisons among different mutual funds and their features. It's a great place to start if you don't know what fund would suit you best.

Vanguard

Website: https://personal.vanguard.com/us/CorporatePortal

American Century

Website: https://www.americancentury.com/index.jsp

T. Rowe Price

Website: https://individual.troweprice.com/public/Retail

Emerging market mutual funds

Templeton Dragon (TDF) – covers Hong Kong, China, and Taiwan

Morgan Stanley Asia-Pacific (APF)

Latin America Equity (LAQ) – covers the whole of Latin America

Korea Fund (KF)

Malaysia Fund (MF)

Singapore Fund (SGF)

Morgan Stanley Emerging Market Fund (EMF)

Insurance comparison

Website: https://www.terms4sale.com

Compares insurance policies according to zip code

A.M. Best's ratings

Tel: 908-439-2200

A.M. Best offers company ratings depending on their performance. Just call them up to find out your company's rating.

Weiss Research

Website: http://www.weissratings.com/

Tel: 800 289 9222

Weiss Research offers objective, consumer-supported reviews of insurance companies.

Bank comparisons

Bankrate.com

Website: http://www.bankrate.com
Bankrate.com is a comparison site for banking services, typically mortgages and bank Certificates of Deposit (CDs). The banks and credit unions used by this comparison site all offer deposits insured by the Federal Deposit Insurance Corporation.

Government securities

Bureau of the Public Debt
Website: http://www.publicdebt.treas.gov
The bureau provides information about buying government securities such as Treasury Bills, note bonds, and US Savings Bonds.

Treasury Direct
Website: http://www.treasurydirect.gov
Treasury Direct is the place to buy government securities such as T-Bills, government bonds, and US Savings Bonds.

Tax

IRS
Website: http://www.irs.gov/
The IRS is the US government agency responsible for tax collection. Visit the website to file a tax return, to download forms, and to get help and advice.

Printed in Great Britain
by Amazon